ROMAN LEGENDS FOR KIDS:

Emperors, Gladiators, History, Myths & More from Ancient Rome

History Brought Alive

Contents

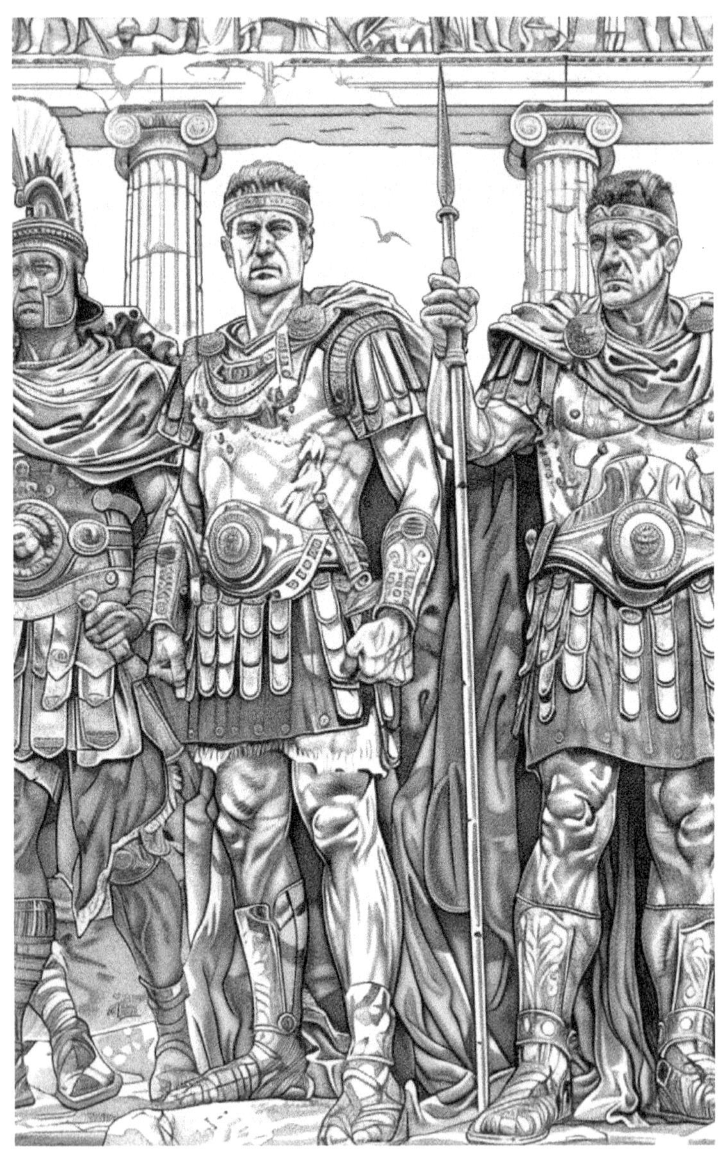

INTRODUCTION

Imagine stepping back thousands of years in time to the grand and bustling empire of Rome. An era of mighty emperors and powerful women, heroic gladiators, and lofty gods, each playing a part in crafting a civilization that shaped our world   today. It's a journey that might seem overwhelming, as the history is packed with events and characters that may feel as distant as the stars. But don't worry! This is the perfect guide to make this ancient world come to life right before your eyes.

We'll march with Julius Caesar as he expands Rome's borders, stand in awe of Cleopatra, cheer for the brave gladiators fighting in the Colosseum, and ascend Mount Olympus to meet with the gods and goddesses of Rome.

Here's a sneak peek of what you'll explore inside:

- **Chapter 1: Mighty Emperors of Rome** — From Julius Caesar's nearly successful grab for ultimate power to Constantine's establishment of a new capital, witness the rise and fall of Rome's greatest leaders.

- **Chapter 2: Powerful Women of Rome** — Discover the stories of the empire's strongest women, who influenced the male-dominated realms of politics and power.

- **Chapter 3: Brave Gladiators of the Colosseum** — Enter the arena to experience the gladiatorial games that captivated Roman citizens, from the lowest commoners to the most noble senators.

- **Chapter 4: Mighty Gods & Goddesses of Rome** — Climb the steps to Mount Olympus, where gods and goddesses like Jupiter, Minerva, and Venus shaped the fates of humans below.

- **Chapter 5: Heroes, Legends & Myths That Shaped Rome** — Discover myths and legends like the founding of the city by Romulus and Remus or the noble sacrifices of heroes like Mucius Scaevola.

We don't just want to tell you these stories but to transport you back in time. You'll feel the excitement, the curiosity, and the drama as if you were a Roman yourself. These are more than simple stories; they are windows into how the ancient Romans lived, thought, and influenced the world around them. These stories teach us lessons that are still relevant today.

So, are you ready for an adventure like no other? Then it's time to turn the page and dive into "Roman Legends for Kids." Let's start our journey through history right now!

(Pay attention to the tales and facts—see if you can become an expert on ancient Rome when you reach the end!)

CHAPTER 1:
MIGHTY EMPERORS OF ROME

Welcome! In this opening chapter, we will step back in time to meet some of the most influential leaders of the ancient Roman Empire. From the wise Augustus, who founded the Empire, to the bold Constantine, who reshaped it entirely, these emperors crafted the history of Rome with their decisions, battles, and laws.

Get ready to explore the lives, accomplishments, and, sometimes, scandals of Rome's greatest emperors. Discover how they came to power, ruled, and the impact of their legacies today.

Julius Caesar | The Almost-Emperor (49 BC - 44 BC)

In the grand, busy world of ancient Rome, full of soldiers in shiny armor and senators in flowing robes, there lived a man who would change everything. His name was Julius Caesar. While he never wore the golden crown of an emperor, his daring actions and clever mind paved the way for those mighty rulers who came after him.

Early Life of a Future Legend

Julius Caesar was born into a time when Rome was a republic, meaning people voted for leaders to make decisions together. But Caesar's family was noble; they were related to heroes of Roman myths! From the time he was just a boy, Caesar knew he was meant for greatness. He was clever and always the first to raise his hand in class. He loved learning about the history of his powerful city.

As a young man, Caesar left Rome to explore the world. He joined the army and traveled far from home, from the sun-baked hills of Spain to the mysterious forests of Germany. Everywhere he went, Caesar fought bravely and thought quickly, earning medals and the respect of his men. But Caesar wanted more than just adventures; he wanted to lead. So, when he returned home, he set his eyes on the biggest prize of all—becoming the leader of Rome.

The Conquest of Gaul

One of Caesar's most famous adventures was in Gaul. Gaul was a region of Western Europe. This was not just a quick battle— it was long and exhausting and lasted several years. Caesar was not only fighting fierce warriors but also the harsh weather and tough terrain. However, with his skills in strategy and bravery, Caesar won many battles. He added vast lands to Rome's territories. Back home, people celebrated his victories with parades and parties, and cheered his name in the streets.

But, not everyone was happy with Caesar's success. Some powerful people in Rome thought he was becoming too influential. They ordered him to come back to Rome without his army and give up his power. Caesar faced a difficult choice at the river Rubicon, which was the border of Italy. Roman law said no general could cross it with an army, or it would mean declaring war on Rome itself.

On a chilly morning, standing by the Rubicon, Caesar made a decision that would change history. He whispered, "The die is cast," and led his army across the river, into Italy. This started a civil war. Caesar knew there was no turning back.

After many battles, Caesar won the civil war. He entered Rome not as a criminal, but as its ruler. He became a dictator, but not the kind we think of today with absolute power. Caesar made many changes during his rule. He gave land to the poor, made laws that were fairer to everyone, and introduced a new calendar, which is the basis for the calendar we use today!

The Ides of March and Caesar's Legacy

Caesar's story doesn't have a happy ending. In 44 BC, on the 15th of March—a day now known as the Ides of March—some of the senators who feared losing their power betrayed him. This day marked the end of Caesar's life, but not his influence. His actions and ideas laid the foundation for the emperors who would follow, starting with his adopted son, Augustus, the first official emperor of Rome.

Julius Caesar's life was like a grand play filled with adventure, danger, and big decisions. Though he never became emperor, his spirit and rules shaped the future of Rome and created a path for emperors to come. His story teaches us about courage, wisdom, and the impact one person can have on the world.

So, remember Julius Caesar, the almost-emperor who dreamed big and dared even bigger.

Augustus | Founder of the Roman Empire (27 BC - AD 14)

In the ancient city of Rome, filled with grand marble buildings, bustling markets, and chariots zipping down the cobblestone streets, there lived an emperor who would forever change history. His name was Augustus, and he was the first emperor of the Roman Empire. From his bold changes to government to grand building projects, Augustus's story is filled with adventure and great achievements.

Augustus was born in 63 BC, during a time of many changes in Rome. His name was originally Gaius Octavius. After

Julius Caesar was betrayed and murdered, young Octavius discovered that Caesar had adopted him as his son. This was a huge surprise to everyone, including Octavius, who was just a teenager at the time. So, he changed his name to Gaius Julius Caesar Octavianus, often called Octavian, stepping into big shoes at a very young age.

Octavian was smart and understood that he needed to act carefully to claim his inheritance. He formed an alliance with Mark Antony, one of Caesar's closest allies, and Marcus Lepidus, a powerful politician. Together, they defeated Caesar's assassins, but it wasn't long before the alliance broke apart. Octavian and Mark Antony became rivals.Their friendship turned into a fierce competition for control of Rome.

The rivalry between Octavian and Mark Antony came to a head in a naval battle at Actium in 31 BC. Octavian's forces defeated Antony's, because Octavian had allied himself with the enchanting Queen Cleopatra of Egypt. This victory was a turning point for Rome. It marked the end of the Roman Republic and the beginning of the Roman Empire.

Augustus, Emperor of Rome

In 27 BC, the Roman Senate changed Octavian's name to Augustus, which means "the respected one." He was now the emperor of Rome. As emperor, Augustus wanted to make Rome into a powerful, organized, and splendid city.

Augustus used to say that he found Rome built of bricks and left it covered in marble. He rebuilt much of the city, adorning it with splendid buildings, statues, and temples that glistened in the sun. Augustus's Rome became a place where art and culture flourished alongside politics and power.

Augustus knew that to build a strong empire, he needed more than just beautiful buildings. He dramatically enlarged the empire, bringing peace and stability to regions that had seen chaos for generations. He reformed the Roman system of taxation to make it fairer and more efficient. Augustus also helped fund grand projects.

He also developed a network of roads that crisscrossed the empire. With the roads, Augustus created a sort of ancient post office system, making communication across long distances faster than ever. This network helped manage the empire and spread Roman culture and influence.

The Founder of the Praetorian Guard

To protect himself and the city, Augustus established the "Praetorian Guard." The members were elite soldiers who served as the personal bodyguards of the emperor, official police and fire fighters.The city became safer and more organized than it had been in years.

Under Augustus's rule, Rome now had a permanent army. The soldiers were ready to defend Rome's borders or expand its territories at a moment's notice.

A Legacy of Peace and Prosperity

Augustus ruled for over 40 years, and his time as emperor was marked by peace and prosperity. This was a period known as the *Pax Romana* or "Roman Peace." He created a strong government that would guide Rome through many more centuries of history.

When Augustus died in AD 14, he left behind an empire that was vastly different from the troubled republic he had inherited. His legacy is not just in the buildings and statues that dotted Rome but the idea of how to run an empire.Through Augustus's story, we see how courage, intelligence, dreams, and a great heart can bring about change and create a legacy that lasts forever.

Tiberius | The Steady Hand of Rome (AD 14 - 37)

Tiberius's story is full of battles, big decisions, and the heavy weight of a crown. As the second emperor of Rome, following his famous stepfather Augustus, Tiberius had big sandals to fill. He was a quiet man, but don't let that fool you—he was also one of Rome's greatest generals and a smart leader.

From Young Soldier to Emperor

Tiberius was born into a noble family in 42 BC, a time when Rome was still figuring out whether it wanted to be a republic or an empire. As a boy, Tiberius learned how to fight and lead soldiers, which was a good thing to know in those days of constant battles.

When he grew up, Tiberius became a famous general. He marched his armies across large parts of Europe, conquering lands and peoples for Rome. He fought in places like Pannonia, Dalmatia, and Raetia, and even ventured into the wild forests of Germania. These conquests helped Rome secure its borders and made Tiberius a hero back home.

Chosen as Successor

Although Tiberius was a great warrior, he didn't jump straight into being an emperor. At first, Augustus wasn't sure who should become the next emperor. But after other possible successors passed away, Augustus picked Tiberius. To prepare Tiberius, Augustus let Tiberius co-lead the empire for a while..

When Tiberius finally became emperor in AD 14, it wasn't easy. The Senate wasn't too happy about having an emperor. They missed the old days when they had more power. Tiberius found it hard to get along with them, and he was always worried that they wanted his crown.

Despite these troubles, Tiberius was really good at his job. He made sure that Rome was well-run, its money well-spent, and its borders secure. He wasn't the kind to spend all day throwing parties or parades; instead, he spent his free time working hard at his job.

Tiberius ruled Rome until AD 37. During this time, he showed that an emperor could be a great general and a careful leader, even if it wasn't always exciting or dramatic.

Tiberius's story is a reminder that being in charge isn't always about glory and fame. Sometimes, it's about doing the hard work behind the scenes, making tough decisions, and looking after a great empire. Thanks to Tiberius's efforts, Rome stayed strong and secure, ready for the many emperors who would come after him.

Caligula | The Wild Emperor (AD 37 - 41)

Caligula is one of Rome's most legendary rulers for all the wrong reasons.His real name was Gaius Julius Caesar Augustus Germanicus. He was called Caligula, which means "little boot," because as a little boy he wore a tiny soldier's outfit, including boots, that the army loved. He became emperor in AD 37, after the death of his grand-uncle and adoptive grandfather, Tiberius.

When Caligula first became emperor, the people of Rome were hopeful. He was young, energetic, and ready to lead. He promised to be a fair ruler, different from Tiberius, who was unpopular by the end of his time.

Caligula started his rule with good deeds. He freed people who had been unjustly imprisoned and got rid of some unfair taxes. He held magnificent games for the entertainment of the citizens, which made him popular. Everyone in Rome was talking about the wonderful new emperor who seemed like a breath of fresh air.

However, things began to change about six months into his rule. Caligula got very sick and was not the same when he recovered. He started doing strange and mean things. He began spending money wildly to build himself huge palaces and stage more extravagant games that emptied the empire's treasury.

Caligula's behavior became more and more unpredictable. He forced Romans to pay heavy taxes to fund his lifestyle.

When he needed more money, he accused rich citizens of crimes, took their properties, and sometimes even ordered their execution. Caligula even said that he was a god! He wanted to put statues of himself in temples across Rome.

Caligula also had a bad relationship with the Roman Senate. He thought that many senators were untrustworthy and wanted his crown. To protect himself, he had several senators executed.

Caligula's strange behavior didn't stop at being mean; he also had some very weird ideas. He once decided to build a bridge made of boats across the Bay of Baiae so he could ride his horse across it wearing the armor of Alexander the Great (who was a famous Greek king and general). He also talked about giving his favorite horse, Incitatus, one of the highest positions in the Roman government as a consul.

The End of His Rule

Caligula didn't last long as emperor because he made too many enemies. In AD 41, after only four years as emperor, one of his bodyguards killed him. The people of Rome, who had once been so hopeful, were happy to get rid of such a wild and unpredictable ruler.

Caligula's time as emperor serves as a reminder that power can be tricky. It shows that it is important for leaders to be kind and fair to everyone. Caligula started with the promise of greatness but will always be remembered for how he became crazy and heartless.

Claudius | The Unexpected Emperor (AD 41 - 54)

One of Rome's most surprising emperors was Tiberius Claudius Caesar Augustus Germanicus, who we will just call Claudius. His effective leadership style was surprising to everyone, and his reign from AD 41 to AD 54 was full of unexpected successes and strange twists of fate.

Though Claudius was born into a royal family, no one expected he would become emperor. He had a tough childhood due to several physical ailments, like tremors in his head and hands, a limp, and other issues that made his own family doubt him. They thought he was too weak to rule such a vast empire, and often made fun of him. However, Claudius would prove them all wrong.

Unlike many of his predecessors, Claudius didn't rush into the chaotic world of Roman politics. He entered the scene relatively late in life, spending much of his younger years out of the public eye, often lost in his books and studies. He was an accomplished historian and a scholar who loved learning about the past.

Claudius became emperor quite unexpectedly after the assassination of the notorious Caligula, his nephew. The Praetorian Guard, aka Rome's elite military force, found

Claudius hiding behind a curtain in the palace during the chaos that followed Caligula's death. Seeing an opportunity, they declared him emperor, thinking they could control him easily. This decision would lead to significant changes in the empire.

Expanding the Empire

One of Claudius's greatest achievements was the expansion of Rome's territories. He completed the Roman annexation of Britain, something other emperors failed to achieve. His military campaigns in Britain were so successful that they added a vast new province to the Roman Empire. This secured Claudius's fame as a conqueror.

He also pushed Rome's borders into parts of Africa and the Middle East, making the empire larger and more diverse than ever before. Under his rule, Rome's influence and power grew significantly.

Reforms and Rights

Claudius was not just a conqueror; he was also a wise leader who made many improvements to the empire. He updated the judicial system to make it more fair, passed laws to protect workers, and extended Roman citizenship to more people. He gave citizens new rights that helped improve their lives, showing that he

cared about his people and their well-being.

Love of Games and Personal Struggles

Claudius loved the Roman games, which were grand events featuring gladiators and wild beasts. These games were not just entertainment; they were a way for the emperor to connect with his people and show off Rome's prosperity.

However, Claudius's personal life was not as successful as his public life. He was notoriously unlucky in love, with several troubled marriages that ended in scandal and tragedy.

The way Claudius died is still a mystery. Some say he was poisoned by his own wife, who wanted her son to become the next emperor. Others think it might have been a sudden illness.

His death marked the end of a surprisingly effective reign that had seen Rome grow stronger and more organized. Despite being underestimated by almost everyone in his early life, Claudius showed that being a good emperor involves more than just looking strong. It's about making smart decisions, caring for your people, and sometimes, surprising everyone by turning weakness into strength.

Claudius expanded an empire, reformed laws, and left a legacy that historians still praise today. He's a reminder that sometimes, the most unlikely person can become a truly mighty leader.

Nero | The Emperor and the Great Fire (AD 54 - 68)

Nero ruled from AD 54 to AD 68. His famous reign was filled with tales of mystery, music, and a very big fire.

Nero became emperor when he was a teenager, stepping into power after the death of his stepfather, Claudius. He was the last emperor of the family line that had started with Augustus. Nero started out well enough with guidance from his advisors, but as he grew older, his rule took a turn for the worse.

In the beginning, Nero was popular. He reduced taxes and gave more power to the Senate, which gave people hope. He loved arts and sports, especially music and chariot racing. Nero wasn't just a fan; he was also a performer who often played the lyre and sang, though it's not clear if he was any good.

Trouble Begins

As Nero got more comfortable in his role, his decisions became more and more controversial. He spent a huge amount of money on arts and building projects, including a massive palace for himself called the Golden House. Manypeople who thought this spending was too extravagant. Nero also did some bad things, like the assassinations of people he didn't trust, including his own mother and his wife. These actions made many people in Rome start to fear and distrust him.

The Great Fire of Rome

One of the most famous events during Nero's time as emperor was the Great Fire of Rome in AD 64. This huge fire lasted for several days and destroyed a large part of the city. Rumors flew around that Nero had played his lyre and sang while Rome burned, although this is probably just a myth. What is true is that after the fire, Nero built his new palace where some of the city had been, which made people even more suspicious that he had let the fire burn on purpose.

Despite the rumors, Nero tried to help the city recover. He opened his palaces to give shelter to those who lost their homes and arranged for food supplies to be distributed. He also made new fire safety laws to try to prevent a similar disaster.

Nero is also known for his harsh treatment of Christians. He blamed them for the Great Fire, among other things. Under his orders, many Christians were persecuted. This was one of many reasons he became unpopular in the empire.

As the years went by, Nero's rule faced increasing problems. Rebellions started in the provinces, and eventually, the Roman Senate turned against him. In AD 68, the Senate declared him to be an enemy of the state. Nerois discovered that even his guards had turned on him, so he took his own life and ended his controversial reign.

Nero's legacy is a mix of good and bad. He was a patron of the arts and a performer, which showed his love for culture. However, his name is often remembered for the negative aspects of his rule—his extravagance, his ruthless actions, and the great fire. His life serves as a reminder of how power can be both a gift and a curse, depending on how it is used.

Vespasian | The Builder of Rome (AD 69 - 79)

Nero's death did not slow down the busy world of ancient Rome. Instead, a new emperor, Vespasian, replaced Nero. He brought peace and grand buildings to the empire. His story is a great adventure filled with challenges and victories, showing us how a strong leader can make a big difference.

Vespasian was born into a family that wasn't particularly famous or powerful, which was unusual for an emperor. He climbed the ranks of the Roman army and became known for his skill as a general. In AD 69, after a year of chaos known as the "Year of the Four Emperors," where four different leaders tried to claim the throne, Vespasian took over. This was a big job, especially after such a turbulent time.

One of the first things Vespasian did as emperor was to stabilize Rome's shaky finances. He was practical and made smart changes to how taxes were collected, which helped fill Rome's empty treasury. He also cut back on unnecessary spending, making sure that the money was used for important things that would help everyone in the empire.

But Vespasian didn't just save money; he also knew when to spend it wisely. He launched a huge building program across Rome, which included some spectacular projects that we can still see ruins of today. The most famous of these is the Colosseum, a giant amphitheater where people watched gladiator fights and other events. It was Vespasian's idea to build a place where Romans could gather for entertainment, bringing joy and pride to his people.

He also built the Temple of Peace and restored the Capitol, which had been damaged by fires during the chaos before he became emperor. These buildings weren't just beautiful; they were symbols of Rome's strength and stability.

With Vespasian in charge, the empire also enjoyed a period of peace and consolidation. This means he worked hard to strengthen the areas Rome already controlled, rather than trying to conquer new lands. This strategy helped make the empire more secure and allowed the people to prosper.

Vespasian was known for being down-to-earth and having a good sense of humor, which helped him connect with people from all walks of life. He often joked about his own policies and even made fun of himself! That was quite unusual for an emperor, but it made him quite popular.

Vespasian ruled for ten years. When he passed away in AD 79, he left behind a stronger, more stable Rome than the one he had inherited. He was succeeded by his sons, who continued his good work, especially in building projects like the Colosseum, which was completed after his death.

Vespasian is remembered as a wise and practical leader who valued peace and stability. He showed that being a good leader isn't just about winning battles or having a famous family; it's also about making smart decisions and caring for your people, and making the world a better place.

Vespasian's story is a great chapter in the tale of Rome's mighty emperors. So, next time you see a picture of the Colosseum, remember Vespasian—the emperor who gifted it to his people as a sign of peace and fun for everyone.

Titus | The Emperor of Good Deeds (AD 79 - 81)

After Vespasian's reign, which focused on stability and the prosperity of the people, a new emperor took the stage. His name was Titus. Although he ruled for just two years, from AD 79 to AD 81, his reign was as brief as it was bright.. Let's dive into the story of this fascinating leader.

Titus was the son of the Colosseum's creator. As a young prince, Titus learned how to lead by watching his father and helping him with important duties. He was a skilled soldier and a smart thinker, which made him a good choice to become emperor after his father.

When Vespasian passed away, Titus took over. At first, people weren't sure if they liked him. They remembered some of the not-so-nice things he had done when he was younger, like destroying a great temple in Jerusalem during a war. But Titus was about to prove everyone wrong.

A Time of Tragedy

Just as Titus was getting started as emperor, a huge disaster struck. Mount Vesuvius, a big volcano near the city of Pompeii, erupted in AD 79. This was the same year Titus became emperor. It was one of the biggest eruptions in history, and it buried the cities of Pompeii and Herculaneum under ash and lava. The eruption trapped thousands of people.

Instead of sitting back in the palace, Titus acted quickly. He sent help to the survivors and spent a lot of money to support the rescue and rebuilding efforts. He showed that he cared deeply about his people's suffering, and this made him very popular.

The Emperor of Good Deeds

During his short time as emperor, Titus did many kind things. He finished building the Colosseum and opened it with grand games that lasted for 100 days. These first games were free for everyone to enjoy!

Elephants, tigers, and gladiators entertained the crowds. Titus often joined the people to watch the games, cheering and laughing along with them. Titus also made laws that were fair and tried to make life better for the ordinary people of Rome. He used the empire's money wisely, to help those in need rather than just making the rich richer.

Mysterious End

Sadly, Titus's time as emperor was very short. He died suddenly after only two years in power, probably from a fever. Some people wondered if his brother, Domitian, who was next in line for the throne, might have had something to do with his death.But, no one knows for sure what happened.

Even though he was emperor for just a little while, Titus is remembered as one of the "good emperors." He showed that being a leader isn't just about power and glory; it's also about taking care of your people when they need help the most.

Titus's story teaches us that you can make a big difference even in a short time. He used his days as emperor to spread joy and help those in need, leaving behind memories of a ruler who truly cared. His legacy is like a shooting star— bright, beautiful, and remembered long after it's gone. This makes him a special chapter in the book of Rome's mighty emperors, teaching us about the power of good deeds and a kind heart.

Domitian | The Builder of Rome's Glory (AD 81 - 96)

In the colorful tapestry of Rome's history, woven with stories of heroes and emperors, one figure stands out for his long reign and big projects. His name was Domitian, who took over after his older brother died suddenly. He was emperor from AD 81 to AD 96. During his 15 years as leader, Domitian worked hard to make Rome a strong and shining capital, even though he was often misunderstood by his people.

When Domitian became emperor after Titus's sudden death, he had big shoes to fill. Unlike his brother, Domitian was serious and private. Because of this, some Romans didn't trust him. But Domitian had great plans for the empire, and he was determined to see them through.

Domitian took over at a time when Rome needed a strong hand. The city had suffered from fires and other disasters, and the empire's borders were always threatened by enemies. Domitian rolled up his sleeves and got to work, making sure Rome was safe and strong.

One of the first things Domitian did was to fix the economy. The money in Rome had been losing its value, which made everything more expensive for the people. Domitian introduced new coins that were worth more and made sure that everyone knew they could trust this new money. This helped everyone from bakers to soldiers buy what they needed without worrying about their coins being worthless.

Domitian loved architecture and believed that a beautiful city was a strong city. He started a massive building program all over Rome. He repaired temples, built new statues, and improved the roads. One of his biggest projects was rebuilding the Capitol, which was an important temple that had been damaged by fire. Under Domitian's orders, Rome began to sparkle again, filled with marvelous buildings that awed everyone who saw them.

But Domitian didn't just focus on the inside of the empire; he also looked outwards to its borders. He knew that safe borders meant a safe Rome. Domitian strengthened the defenses along the empire's edges, building forts and training soldiers to make sure that no enemies could sneak in. These efforts kept the people inside the empire safe and made Domitian popular with the soldiers.

A Controversial Figure

Even though he did many good things for Rome, Domitian wasn't very popular with the Senate. They thought Domitian wanted too much power for himself. This tension made it difficult for him to rule, and many senators did not trust him.

Unfortunately, the distrust of the Senate and others that surrounded him led to a sad end for Domitian. In AD 96, after 15 years of ruling, Domitian was betrayed and assassinated in a palace conspiracy. His death marked the end of the Flavian dynasty, which included his father, Vespasian, and his brother, Titus.

Domitian shows us that being a leader isn't always about being popular; it's about making tough decisions that can help people in the long run. His story teaches us about the importance of having goals as a leader. Domitian reminds us that even the most misunderstood rulers can have a positive impact on history.

Trajan | The Great Builder and Conqueror (AD 98 - 117)

Domitian's successor, the emperor Trajan, stands out as one of the greatest. Ruling from AD 98 to AD 117, Trajan was known for his kindness, his love for building, and his adventurous spirit through the expansion of Rome's borders.

Trajan was born in a place called Hispania, which is now part of Spain, which made him the first Roman emperor born outside of Italy. This gave him a unique perspective and helped him connect with many different people across the vast empire. Before he became emperor, Trajan was a famous general who won many battles and earned the respect of his soldiers and the people.

When Trajan took the throne in AD 98, he decided to make Rome even greater. He was a fair and wise ruler. The people loved him due to his fairness. He also made Rome a stable and prosperous place. Unlike some emperors who only wanted power for themselves, Trajan truly cared about the well-being of his citizens.

A Vast Building Program

Trajan loved architecture. He believed that building impressive structures could make Rome even more glorious. He started a vast building program that saw the creation of new roads, bridges, and buildings all over the empire. One of his most famous projects was "Trajan's Market," which was like a big shopping mall where people could buy all sorts of goods. It was a bustling place where traders from all over the empire came together.

One of the most amazing things Trajan built was "Trajan's Column." This tall column is covered in detailed carvings that tell the story of Trajan's wars in Dacia, which is now the country of Romania. It's similar to a giant comic strip, but made of stone. It shows battles, soldiers, and the people of Dacia. "Trajan's Column" not only celebrated his victories but also served as a reminder of how he expanded the empire and his legacy.

Expanding the Empire

Trajan was not only a builder, but also a great conqueror. He believed that Rome needed to expand to become stronger. Under his rule, the empire was the biggest in history. It stretched from the sands of the Sahara to the rainy lands of Britain, and east to the rich cities of the Middle East. He led his armies with courage and skill, winning territories and securing Rome's borders against its enemies.

What made Trajan truly special was his care for all people throughout the empire. He set up programs to help poor children, giving them food and educating them. This showed that he was both powerful and kind-hearted. Trajan wanted to make sure even the least fortunate could have a good life.

The Legacy of Trajan

Trajan ruled Rome for nearly twenty years. When he died in AD 117, he was deeply mourned by the people. He was called *Optimus Princeps*, which means "the best leader," because he was seen as the ideal emperor. He left behind a stronger, more beautiful Rome.

Trajan's ability to combine the might of a warrior with the heart of a caretaker shows us that being a great leader is about much more than just winning battles; it's about making life better for your people.

Hadrian | The Traveling Emperor (AD 117 - 138)

Emperor Hadrian shines as a unique character. He took over immediately after his adopted father, Trajan, died. He ruled from AD 117 to AD 138. Unlike many emperors who focused on war, Hadrian loved peace, culture, and especially everything Greek! Let's travel back in time and see what made Emperor Hadrian such a memorable leader.

From the start, Hadrian decided to do things a bit differently. He believed that the Roman Empire was big enough. It was time to make sure the people were secure and happy, rather than trying to conquer more lands. This idea made him very popular in some places but not so much in others.

A Lover of Greek Culture

One of Hadrian's biggest passions was his love for Greek culture, which he thought was the best way to learn and live. Greeks had great ideas about art, science, philosophy, and government. Hadrian wanted to spread these ideas throughout his empire. To show his dedication, he even spent a whole year living in Greece. He spent a lot of time in Athens, which was like the New York City of ancient culture!

While living in Athens, Hadrian wasn't just sitting around enjoying the views. He helped make the city even more beautiful and functional. He built new public buildings, such as a fabulous library where people could read and learn, and an aqueduct. Aqueducts served as a kind of water bridge and brought fresh water to the city's people.

Hadrian's most impressive project was finishing the vast Temple of Olympian Zeus, a huge temple that had been under construction for over 500 years! When Hadrian completed it, the temple was one of the largest and most stunning in all of Greece, showing how much he adored and respected Greek culture.

Hadrian didn't just want to build things; he wanted to be a part of Greek life. He joined in religious festivals and rituals, celebrating the gods and goddesses of Greek mythology with the people. This wasn't just for fun; it was a way for Hadrian to show that he was one of them, not just their ruler from afar in Rome.

Hadrian's Wall

Back in the Roman Empire, Hadrian knew that to keep peace he needed strong borders. One of his most famous projects was building Hadrian's Wall across what is now Northern England. This massive wall was meant to keep out invaders and mark the northern limit of his empire. It was so well built that parts of it still stand today!

Under Hadrian's rule, the Roman Empire enjoyed a period of peace and prosperity. He made laws that were fairer. He tried to make sure that governors in different parts of the empire were doing their jobs right and improved the lives of many people. His focus on building and culture brought a lot of beauty and joy to the empire.

Hadrian passed away in AD 138 after a long and eventful reign. He was remembered as a wise and cultured emperor who made the Roman Empire a better place through his understanding and respect for different cultures.

Emperor Hadrian shows us that leadership is also about learning, sharing culture, and making the world more beautiful and safe for everyone. Hadrian's journey as emperor teaches us the importance of celebrating the things that make us all unique.

Antoninus Pius | The Peaceful Emperor (AD 138 - 161)

Antoninus Pius took over after Hadrian, ruling from AD 138 to AD 161. Unlike many emperors before him who spent their days on battlefields, Antoninus Pius preferred to bring peace and happiness to the empire.

Antoninus Pius was born into a noble family and grew up learning about the ways of government and leadership. When Emperor Hadrian chose him as his successor, he knew Antoninus was wise and kind enough to lead Rome well. Upon becoming emperor, Antoninus was given the name Pius because he showed great respect and piety towards Hadrian. Pius honored all Hadrian's wishes, including adopting two young men, Marcus Aurelius and Lucius Verus, who were to become the next emperors after him.

A Time of Peace

What made Antoninus Pius's reign remarkable was how peaceful it was. For 23 years, the Roman Empire saw no major revolts or invasions. It was a golden time when people could focus on their crops, their crafts, and their families without the constant worry of war. This peaceful period allowed Antoninus to improve the lives of his people. He repaired roads and cities, made laws that were fair, and worked hard to ensure that justice was served throughout the empire. He believed that a good emperor must be like a good father, looking after all his citizens with care and fairness.

The Antonine Wall

Even though his reign was peaceful, Antoninus Pius knew the importance of a strong defense. Early in his rule, he ordered the construction of a new wall in southern Scotland, called the Antonine Wall. This wall was built north of Hadrian's Wall. It was meant to protect the Roman Empire from the tribes in the north. It stretched from coast to coast and was fortified with ditches, ramparts, and forts. The Antonine Wall was a massive project and showed the might of Rome even in peaceful times. It was a symbol of how Antoninus Pius extended Roman influence without extensive warfare, preferring strong defenses and clear boundaries.

Life in the Empire under Antoninus Pius

During the time of Antoninus Pius, the Roman Empire flourished. Cities grew larger and markets bustled with traders from all over the world. Artists and philosophers could create and think without the interruptions of war.

Antoninus was also known for his generosity. He used the empire's money to help cities struck by disasters like earthquakes and fires. He believed that the empire's strength didn't just come from its army but from the happiness and health of its people.

Antoninus Pius died in AD 161, leaving behind an empire that was stable and strong. His peaceful approach to ruling was a breath of fresh air in the turbulent history of Rome. He proved that with wise management and a focus on the welfare of the people, an emperor could be just as mighty in peace as in war.

His adopted sons, Marcus Aurelius and Lucius Verus, took over after him, and they continued his policies of careful, thoughtful leadership. Antoninus's reign is often seen as the height of the Roman Empire's peace and prosperity.

Antoninus Pius teaches us that peace, strong borders, and care for the people can lead to a golden age just as much as victory in battle. His wise and gentle rule left a lasting impression on Rome.

Marcus Aurelius | The Philosopher Emperor (AD 161 - 180)

When Marcus Aurelius took over for his adopted father, he ruled with wisdom and power. His reign lasted from AD 161 to AD 180. Marcus wasn't just an emperor; he was also a philosopher who wrote down his thoughts on how to live a good life, which are still read by people around the world today.

Marcus Aurelius was born into a wealthy and important family. From a young age, he was trained in the art of leadership and the studies of philosophy, particularly Stoicism—a type of philosophy that teaches the importance of reason and self-control in facing life's challenges. Stoics believe that a good life comes from doing your duty and accepting your fate with courage. When Marcus became emperor, he continued to live by these lessons. He tried to rule wisely and fairly, and always worked to improve himself and his empire.

Becoming Emperor

Marcus Aurelius and Lucius Verus started by sharing the duties of emperor in AD 161. Together, they ruled over an empire that was peaceful thanks to the efforts of their predecessor, Antoninus Pius. However, Marcus's reign soon faced challenges, including wars on the empire's frontiers and a devastating plague that swept through the land. Despite these troubles, Marcus tried to maintain peace and stability within the Roman Empire. He believed that it was his duty to look after his people and protect them as best he could.

The Philosopher on the Throne

What made Marcus truly unique was his commitment to Stoic philosophy even while being an emperor. He often wrote about his ideas and reflections in a book called *The Meditations*. At first, this wasn't a book meant for others to read—it was his personal diary, filled with notes to himself on how to be a better person and a better leader.

In *The Meditations*, Marcus wrote about the importance of accepting what you can't change and dealing calmly with other people. He wrote that you should always try to do the right thing, no matter how hard it might be. These writings offer a rare glimpse into the mind of an emperor who deeply cared about being moral and fair.

As a leader, Marcus Aurelius was known for his efforts to bring peace whenever possible. He worked hard to protect the empire's borders, but preferred to solve conflicts without fighting. When wars were necessary, he led his soldiers with courage and care, always mindful of the hardships of battle.

Marcus was also fair in his dealings with people from all walks of life. He passed laws to help the poor and made sure that slaves could have a chance to gain their freedom. He believed that all people, no matter their status, deserved respect and justice.

Legacy of a Wise Emperor

When Marcus Aurelius died in AD 180, his death marked the end of the Pax Romana, the long period of relative peace and stability within the Roman Empire. He was succeeded by his son, Commodus, who unfortunately did not share his father's wisdom or commitment to philosophy.

Today, Marcus Aurelius is remembered not just as a powerful emperor, but as a wise and thoughtful philosopher. His life reminds us that being a good leader is about much more than giving orders—it's also about setting an example of how to live a good and meaningful life.

We can learn a lot from Marcus Aurelius, like how to stay calm in tough situations, how to be fair to others, and why it's important to always keep learning and growing…no matter who you are or what challenges you face.

Septimius Severus | The Warrior Emperor (AD 193 - 211)

After the Pax Romana ended, Rome started to face many changes and challenges. During this time, Septimius Severus became emperor. He ruled from AD 193 to AD 211. His story is full of battles, adventures, and big building projects. Let's take a closer look at this fascinating emperor who left a lasting mark on Rome.

Septimius Severus came from the city of Leptis Magna, which is in modern-day Libya. He was the first Roman Emperor from Africa, which made his rise to power quite unique. Severus was known for being a strong and determined leader. He became emperor after winning a civil war against other rivals who also wanted to become emperor.

When Severus became emperor, Rome was going through a turbulent time. He knew he needed to make it clear to everyone in the empire that he was in charge. To do this, he showed both his might as a warrior and his skill as a leader.

The Triumphal Arch

One of the most famous things Severus did was to build a grand arch in the Roman Forum. This wasn't just any arch—it was a triumphal arch, which is a big, decorative structure that celebrates victories in battle. The Arch of Septimius Severus is still standing today, and it tells his story of success as a leader.

This arch was beautifully decorated with carvings that, like a comic book, showed scenes of his victories over the Parthian Empire (modern-day Iran). By building this arch, Severus told everyone that he was a strong emperor who could protect and lead Rome.

Severus also wanted to make sure that his family, the Severan dynasty, would keep ruling Rome after he was gone. So, the arch also served as a way to show that his family was rightful and legitimate, and deserved to be in charge because of their strength and leadership.

Severus made many changes during his reign. He strengthened the army by increasing pay for the soldiers. He made sure they were loyal first to him and then to Rome. He also traveled a lot around the empire, from Britain to Syria, making laws and improving cities wherever he went. In Britain, he fought against the tribes in the north and even tried to strengthen Hadrian's Wall. He wanted to make sure that all parts of the empire were well-protected and governed.

A Family Man

Severus was also a family man. He had two sons, Caracalla and Geta, whom he tried to prepare to rule after him. He wanted them to learn how to be good leaders, just like he was. Unfortunately, his sons didn't get along, and this caused problems later on.

Severus died in AD 211 in the city of York during a battle in Britain. His rule had seen the Roman Empire stabilize and grow stronger after a period of uncertainty. He left behind a legacy of strong military power and impressive architecture, like his famous arch, which people from all over the world still go to see today.

Septimius Severus shows us that a great leader can come from anywhere, and that a ruler looks out not only for his own time but for the future as well. His triumphal arch, still standing in the heart of Rome, reminds us of his power and his legacy, which have lasted through the ages.

Diocletian | The Emperor Who Divided Rome (AD 284 - 305)

Let's jump forward to Emperor Diocletian, who stands out as a mastermind of change. His rule from AD 284 to 305 brought significant reforms that helped stabilize the struggling Roman Empire during tough times. Let's explore how this clever leader made a big difference.

Diocletian was born around AD 245 in the region of Dalmatia (now part of modern Croatia). He rose from humble beginnings, climbing the ranks of the Roman military through determination and skill. His real name was Diocles, but he took the name Diocletian when he became emperor. His leadership came at a time when Rome desperately needed strong hands to guide it.

A Time of Trouble

Before Diocletian became emperor, Rome was going through the "Crisis of the Third Century." This was a difficult period marked by economic problems, invasions, and the empire nearly breaking apart. Multiple emperors came and went, each unable to fix the deep issues facing Rome.

Diocletian had a revolutionary idea: the empire was too big for one person to manage, especially in such chaotic times. So, he decided to split the empire in half. In AD 285, he divided Rome into the Eastern and Western Empires. But Diocletian didn't stop there. He introduced the Tetrarchy, a system where four rulers would share power—two senior emperors called Augusti and two junior emperors called Caesars.

Diocletian ruled the Eastern part of the empire, which included the wealthier provinces that were less troubled by invasions. This decision helped each part of the empire get the attention it needed to manage its specific problems, making governing more efficient and effective.

Reforms and Recovery

Under Diocletian's rule, the empire saw major improvements. He reorganized the government to make it more structured. This way, the emperors could better serve the people and handle crises. He also reformed the economy by introducing new coins to replace the old, less valuable ones.

To strengthen the military, Diocletian increased the number of soldiers and built stronger defenses along the empire's borders. These actions helped protect the empire from outside attacks and brought more stability.

For ordinary people, Diocletian's reign brought mixed feelings. On one hand, his economic reforms eventually led to higher taxes, which some people found difficult. On the other hand, the empire was becoming more stable, and there were fewer invasions disrupting their lives.

Diocletian's Retirement: A Historic First

Diocletian did something no Roman emperor had done before; he retired, which shocked everyone. In AD 305, after 21 years as emperor, he decided to step away from power. He believed that fresh leadership could bring new ideas and keep the empire strong. Diocletian spent his last years in a palace he built in his homeland, enjoying a quiet life away from the stress of ruling.

Diocletian's reforms set the stage for a more organized and stable empire, even though the peace didn't last forever. The Tetrarchy eventually broke down, leading to new conflicts, but his ideas about dividing the empire influenced future leaders, including Constantine the Great.

Emperor Diocletian teaches us that sometimes solving big problems requires bold, new ideas. His decision to split the empire and share power showed that teamwork and smart planning can help solve even the toughest issues. Diocletian's story is a chapter in Roman history that highlights the importance of adaptability and innovation in leadership.

Constantine | The Great (AD 306 - 337)

In the grand story of the Roman Empire, Emperor Constantine the Great shines as one of the most transformative figures. He ruled from AD 306 to AD 337, making decisions that reshaped the empire's spiritual landscape and founded a city that would stand as a beacon of power for centuries. Let's step back in time and discover the life of this remarkable leader.

Constantine was born in the year AD 272, in a region that is now part of Serbia. His father was a powerful Roman officer who would become emperor. So, Constantine grew up in the emperor's courts, learning the arts of leadership and war. When his father died in AD 306, Constantine was declared emperor by his father's troops.

The Path to Power

Becoming emperor was just the beginning for Constantine. When his reign began, the Roman Empire was not united under one leader but was divided among several, leading to a period of chaos and conflict. Constantine had to fight a series of battles against these other rulers to secure his position as the sole emperor. The most famous of these battles was the Battle of the Milvian Bridge in AD 312.

Before the Battle of the Milvian Bridge, Constantine experienced a profound moment that would define his rule. According to stories, on the night before the battle he saw a sign in the sky. It was a cross made of light. He also saw the words, "In this sign, you will conquer." Believing this to be a divine message, Constantine had his soldiers paint the Christian symbol on their shields. After winning, Constantine attributed his success to the Christian God.

A New Religious Path for Rome

After his victory, Constantine made a big decision: he would support Christianity, a religion whose followers had been persecuted under previous Roman emperors. In AD 313, he issued the Edict of Milan, which granted religious freedom to Christians and allowed them to worship openly. This paved the way for Christianity to become the empire's dominant faith.

Constantine's vision extended beyond religion. He saw the need for a new capital city that could reflect his riches and the empire's renewed strength. Thus, he founded Constantinople in AD 330 on the site of the ancient city of Byzantium.

Constantinople was strategically located on the crossroads between Europe and Asia. It was a vibrant hub for trade and culture. Massive walls helped to protect the city that was filled with grand palaces and decorated with splendid churches. Constantinople would later become known as one of the most powerful cities in the world. It became the capital of the Byzantine Empire long after the fall of the Western Roman Empire.

Legacy of a Visionary

Constantine ruled until his death in AD 337. His reign marked a significant turning point in the history of the West, as he transformed the Roman Empire in ways that still resonate today. Constantine was significant in both establishing Christianity as a major world religion as well as laying the foundation for what would become the Byzantine Empire.

Constantine the Great was more than just a conqueror; he was a visionary who redefined the ancient world. His story teaches us about the power of faith and the importance of bold leadership.

Theodosius I | The Great Peacemaker (AD 379 - 395)

The next significant ruler after Constantine was Theodosius I, who holds a special place in the history of Roman emperors as a peacemaker. Known as Theodosius the Great, he ruled the Roman Empire from AD 379 to AD 395. He was the last emperor to rule over both the eastern and western parts of the empire (before it split into two separate empires). Let's explore the life of this important leader.

Theodosius was born in Spain around AD 347. He grew up in a time when the Roman Empire was facing many challenges, including attacks from outside groups called "barbarians." Theodosius learned about military strategy and leadership from his father, who was a high-ranking officer in the army. This training prepared him well for the big role he would later take on as emperor.

Becoming Emperor

In AD 379, Theodosius was chosen to be the new emperor of the Eastern Roman Empire after the death of the previous leader. His first big challenge was to deal with a group called the Goths, who were causing trouble in the eastern parts of the empire. The Goths were a powerful group that had moved into Roman territory looking for a new place to live. Previous emperors had tried to push them out with military force, but these attempts had often led to more conflict and problems. Theodosius had a different idea. He decided to make peace with the Goths. So, he allowed them to live within the empire's borders in the territory between the lower Danube and the Balkan mountains. This was a bold move.

Theodosius treated the Goths fairly. He allowed them to have their own leaders and live by their own laws as long as they remained loyal to Rome. This agreement brought peace to the region and showed that different groups could live together under one empire.

As emperor, Theodosius worked hard to keep the empire united. He believed that a strong and united Rome was better for everyone. He made laws that were fair and worked to make sure that people in both the eastern and western parts of the empire felt connected and supported by the government.

Promoting Christianity

Another important part of Theodosius's reign was his support for Christianity. He was a devout Christian and made decisions that helped strengthen the Christian church within the empire. In AD 380, he issued a law that made Christianity the official religion of the Roman Empire. This was a significant change because it meant that Christianity was now the main religion supported by the emperor himself.

Theodosius ruled for 16 years. When he died in AD 395, his two sons inherited different parts of the empire. One son took over the east and the other took the west. This division marked the official split of the Roman Empire into the Eastern Roman Empire and the Western Roman Empire, which would have very different futures.

Theodosius I is remembered as a wise and thoughtful leader who tried to bring peace and stability to a vast and diverse empire. His ability to make peace with the Goths and his efforts to unite the empire under Christianity had long-lasting impacts on the history of Europe. Theodosius shows us that sometimes, making peace can be more powerful than winning a battle.

Chapter conclusion

We've traveled through the reigns of Rome's most formidable emperors, exploring their monumental achievements, their struggles, and the unforgettable marks they left on history. From Augustus's establishment of peace through the Pax Romana to the transformative rule of Constantine, these leaders not only shaped the political landscape of their time but also laid the foundations for modern governance and civilization.

As we conclude this chapter, we reflect on the complex legacy of these rulers—their vision, their power, and their human flaws. Their stories remind us of the profound impact leadership can have on the fate of nations and the course of history.

Now, as we turn the page, we look forward to diving deeper into the rich tapestry of Roman life. We will explore their daily experiences, cultural achievements, and enduring mysteries of one of history's most fascinating civilizations. Let's continue our journey through ancient Rome!

CHAPTER 2:
POWERFUL WOMEN OF ROME

In this chapter, we'll meet some of ancient Rome's most amazing women.. Though men of this time made most of the big decisions, these women found ways to leave their mark on history. From Livia Drusilla, who was smart and a good planner, to Cornelia, a brave mom who raised famous sons, their stories are full of adventure and inspiration. Let's discover how these incredible ladies showed that anyone can make history. Get ready for some exciting tales about Rome's most powerful women!

Livia Drusilla: The Emperor's Confidante (30 January 59 BC – AD 29)

In the ancient city of Rome, there once lived a remarkable woman named Livia Drusilla. In this busy city, Livia stood out. Not just as a queenly figure beside her husband, Emperor Augustus, but as a powerful woman whose whispers could move mountains within the palace walls.

Livia Drusilla was more than just the wife of Augustus; she was his closest advisor, friend, and confidante. When Augustus became the first emperor of Rome, it wasn't just his wisdom that led the empire—it was also Livia's clever counsel. Though women in Rome didn't typically rule openly, Livia found her way to influence. She was like a skilled puppeteer, subtly pulling the strings behind the majestic red curtains of the empire.

Livia used her intelligence and charm to help Augustus make big decisions. From deciding which roads to build, to solving squabbles in the Senate, Livia was always ready with smart ideas. She knew how to play the game of politics just as well as any of the men in government, and sometimes even better!

A Mother Shapes an Emperor

Livia wasn't just important to Rome; she was also a super mom! She had two sons, Tiberius and Drusus. From a young age, Livia had big dreams for Tiberius. She imagined him becoming a great leader, just like his stepfather, Augustus. While Drusus grew up to be a brave general, Livia focused her attention on preparing Tiberius for the ultimate role: Emperor of Rome.

Livia taught Tiberius how to understand what people needed or feared. This wasn't always easy, as Tiberius was shy and serious (unlike the charming Augustus). But under his mother's guidance, Tiberius learned the art of leadership and diplomacy. Livia also arranged for Tiberius to marry someone who would help him boost his popularity and power. These actions made Livia seem like a chess player, as she carefully moved her pieces to ensure Tiberius's path to the throne was clear.

Her plans worked well because eventually, after many years and the sad passing of his younger brother Drusus, Tiberius became emperor. Thanks to Livia's early influence, Tiberius knew how to keep the empire together, even during tough times.

Legacy of a Powerful Matron

Livia Drusilla's story is not just about power and politics; it's about the strength of a woman in a man's world. She showed that being a queen isn't only about wearing a crown; it's about using your mind and heart to make a difference. Livia's influence reminds us that behind every great leader, there might just be a wisewoman with a brave heart.

Agrippina the Younger: Mother of an Emperor (6 November AD 15 – 23 March AD 59)

Next we will step into Emperor Nero's time, where a woman named Agrippina the Younger lived. Agrippina was a fierce and ambitious mother who would stop at nothing to see her son, Nero, rise as emperor. Let's embark on a journey through her thrilling and dramatic life!

Agrippina was born into a family that was very close to the throne. So, her family was no stranger to power, as her brother was the Emperor Caligula, and her uncle was Claudius. From a young age, Agrippina knew she was meant for greatness.

Agrippina dreamed not just of standing beside powerful men, but of holding power herself. As she grew up, Agrippina became known for her sharp mind and fearless spirit. Like Livia, Agrippina could be compared to a chess player. She made very calculated moves, thinking many steps ahead of everyone else. But her ultimate goal was to see her son Nero wear the emperor's purple robe—a symbol of supreme power in Rome.

The Master Plan

When Agrippina married her uncle Claudius, who was emperor at that time, many people in Rome whispered behind closed doors. They were shocked because it was unusual and a bit scandalous. But for Agrippina, this was a strategic move. As the wife of the emperor, she had a direct path to guide her young son Nero toward the throne.

Agrippina worked hard to position Nero as the next emperor. She persuaded Claudius to adopt Nero and make him heir. This meant that Claudius pushed aside his own son, Britannicus. Agrippina made sure that when this chess game ended, her son, Nero, would shout "checkmate!" as he took the throne.

As expected, Agrippina's clever planning paid off. When Claudius died under mysterious circumstances (some say Agrippina might have plotted against him), Nero became emperor, meaning that Agrippina's dream came true! She was the mother of the emperor and the most powerful woman in Rome. But, as in many tales of power and ambition, reaching the top was not the end of Agrippina's story.

Getting to the top can be tricky, but staying there can be even trickier. Nero, once a puppet in his mother's hands, started to grow up and wanted to rule on his own. He didn't like his mother controlling every move he made. Like a bird that wants to fly after learning how to use its wings, Nero wanted to be free from his mother's tight grip.

As Nero asserted his independence, Agrippina lost her influence. The once unbreakable bond between mother and son began to crack. In a dramatic turn of events, their relationship ended tragically. Nero, feeling threatened by his mother's power, decided there was only one way to keep his throne secure—to have Agrippina removed. In a dark twist of fate, Nero ordered his own mother to be taken away, never to be seen again.

Remembering Agrippina

Agrippina the Younger's story is a powerful reminder of the heights to which ambition can soar and the depths to which it can fall. She was a woman who played the political game as cunningly as any great leader of her time. She showed the world that a woman, too, could orchestrate the rise of emperors and shape the course of history.

Julia Domna: Philosopher and Empress (170 AD-217 AD)

After discussing Agrippina, who got as close to ruling Rome as possible through her son, we will move onto someone who became an empress. Her name is Julia Domna. Julia was not only a queen but also a philosopher, a mother, and a political strategist. Her story is one of intellect and influence, showing that the power of the mind can be just as mighty as the power of an army.

The Empress Who Loved to Think

Julia Domna was born in Syria, far from the bustling streets of Rome. She was known for her brilliant mind and love for philosophy. Philosophy is all about thinking deeply about life's big questions—such as what is right and wrong and how we should treat others. Julia believed that understanding these big ideas was just as important as any treasure.

When she married Septimius Severus, who would become one of Rome's greatest emperors, she moved to Rome, bringing her love of learning with her. As empress, Julia was not content to sit quietly in her palace; instead, she created a gathering place for some of the smartest thinkers of the day. Imagine a place where every room buzzes with ideas, and poets, philosophers, and scholars debate under glittering chandeliers. That was Julia's palace!

A Queen in the World of Politics

Julia's influence didn't stop at philosophical discussions. She was deeply involved in the politics of Rome, advising her husband on important decisions. When Septimius Severus went on military campaigns to expand the empire, Julia was right there with him. She didn't just act as his supportive wife, but also a crucial advisor. She showed that a queen could be just as savvy and strategic as her king, steering the empire through times of war and peace.

Her role as a political advisor didn't just make her popular—it made her essential. Julia Domna was like the coach of a team. Her husband was the captain, and the empire was their field. She helped plan their moves and was a key player in the game of empire-building.

Even after her death, the ideas and values that Julia left with her sons and court continued to shape Roman politics and culture. Her intellectual gatherings were remembered as golden moments in Rome's history, where the mind was celebrated alongside the might of the sword.

Julia Domna's life reminds us of the importance of thinking deeply about the world and our place in it. In museums today, we can still see statues of Julia with thoughtful, wise eyes. These statues show us that, long ago, this empress of Rome knew the value of a good question and thoughtful conversation.

So, as you turn the pages of this book and explore more tales of ancient Rome, remember Julia Domna as a philosopher and empress who believed in the power of ideas. Her story shows that even during times of emperors and battles, the pen—or the philosopher's stone—could be just as mighty as the sword!

Boudica: Warrior Queen against Rome

Now, let's travel to the misty, green lands of Britain, where a fierce queen named Boudica lived. Her story is one of courage and defiance, as she stood tall against the mighty Roman Empire. Boudica was not just a queen; she was a warrior, a leader, and a hero to her people. Let's ride with her on her incredible journey against one of the most powerful forces in the ancient world.

The Spark of Revolt

Boudica was the queen of the Iceni tribe in what is now eastern England. The Iceni were proud and strong, living peacefully under their own laws and leaders. However, their peace was shattered when the Romans came. The Romans were like a storm that swept across the land, taking control of everything in their path. They took lands, demanded heavy taxes, and treated the local tribes unfairly.

The trouble truly began when Boudica's husband, the king, died. His wish was that his kingdom would be shared between his daughters and the Roman emperor, hoping to protect his family and people. But the Romans had other ideas. They ignored his wishes, took everything, and treated Boudica and her daughters cruelly. This injustice lit a fire in Boudica's heart, and she promised to fight back.

Leading the Charge

Boudica's spirit and call to arms ignited a fierce desire for freedom among her people and neighboring tribes. She became the leader of a massive rebellion, rallying thousands of warriors to her cause. Boudica was not just fighting for revenge; she was fighting for the freedom of her land and people.

Imagine seeing Boudica in her chariot, red hair blazing, her voice thundering over the crowds, stirring her warriors to battle. She led her army with such courage that even the mighty Romans trembled. Her army marched through cities, reclaiming them from Roman rule. Their message was clear: this land belonged to the Britons, not distant emperors.

The Romans were shocked and scared by the strength of Boudica's uprising. They had thought it would be easy to rule over the Britons, but Boudica proved them wrong. She showed that even the most powerful empire could be challenged by the heart and spirit of those oppressed.

Although Boudica's rebellion was eventually crushed by the well-trained Roman legions, her story did not end there. Her courage made her a legend, a symbol of resistance against tyranny. The tale of Boudica teaches us that standing up for what is right, even in the face of overwhelming odds, is a true hero's path.

Fulvia: A Woman in the Civil War (83 - 40 BC)

After Boudica fought her rebellion, while senators debated in the Forum, there lived a woman of remarkable strength and influence. Her name was Fulvia. She was not like the quiet, reserved women of her time. Instead, Fulvia was a powerful figure in Roman politics, and her life was intertwined with the republic's most turbulent years.

Fulvia and the Game of Politics

Fulvia was not just any Roman matron; rather, she was a political powerhouse. She married three of the most influential men in Rome, each of whom played a pivotal role in the Republic's final years. Her husbands included Publius Clodius Pulcher, a radical politician; Gaius Scribonius Curio, a passionate supporter of Julius Caesar; and finally, Mark Antony, a daring and ambitious leader known for his alliances with Julius Caesar and later, Cleopatra.

During her relationship with Mark Antony, Fulvia became heavily involved in Roman politics. She was not content to stay behind the scenes. Instead, she actively participated in the complex and often messy political arena like a coach whose team was always in the middle of the most important play of the game. She managed estates, rallied troops, and even issued orders, much like a queen in a game of chess, moving her pieces across a board filled with danger and intrigue.

The Perusine War: A Stand Against Octavian

One of Fulvia's most famous—and dramatic—political moves was during the Perusine War. This was not just any conflict; instead, it was a fierce struggle for power between Fulvia (and her brother-in-law, Lucius Antonius) and Octavian, who was Mark Antony's rival and the future emperor Augustus.

So, why did this war start? After Julius Caesar's death, Rome was full of power struggles. And, Fulvia was right in the middle of it all. She felt that Octavian was taking too much power and sidelining Mark Antony, her husband. So, what did Fulvia do? She didn't just stand by; she took action!

Fulvia and Lucius Antonius gathered an army and took control of the city of Perusia (modern-day Perugia in Italy). Imagine her, a woman in a world of soldiers and senators, commanding forces and making strategic decisions. They held the city against Octavian's forces through a harsh winter, showing incredible resilience and determination.

However, the Perusine War did not end well for Fulvia. Octavian's troops eventually broke through, and Fulvia was forced to flee. The war showed Octavian's ruthless side and led to further struggles between him and Mark Antony. Still, the war highlighted Fulvia's incredible courage and her willingness to fight for her family's position in the swirling chaos of Roman politics.

Fulvia's life was a series of battles, not just with swords and shields, but with words, alliances, and wills. She showed that a woman, even in ancient Rome, could wield power in ways that echoed through the halls of history. As you explore more tales of ancient Rome, remember Fulvia not as a figure in the shadows, but rather a blazing force in the spotlight. She was a woman who might have used a stylus more often than a sword but who fought just as fiercely for her place and her principles.

Cornelia Scipionis Africana: Mother of Reformers (c. 190 – 115 BC)

Where Fulvia shone most brightly in her political strategies, another woman proved herself to be extraordinary due to her wisdom and dignity—Cornelia Scipionis Africana. Known not just for her noble birth but for her remarkable role as a mother and mentor, Cornelia's story is one of inspiration and influence. She was the mother of the Gracchi brothers, Tiberius and Gaius, who were famous for their bold reforms in Roman politics.

A Mother's Guidance

Cornelia was born into one of Rome's most important families. Her father was Scipio Africanus, a celebrated general who defeated Hannibal in the Punic Wars. With such a heritage, Cornelia grew up steeped in the values of courage, duty, and public service—values she would, in turn, deeply instill in her own children.

As a mother, Cornelia's most enduring legacy was the education and upbringing she provided to her sons, Tiberius and Gaius Gracchus. She didn't just teach them to read and write; however, she also filled their minds with ideas of justice, equality, and the importance of serving the common people. Imagine a classroom where lessons are about how to improve the world—a place where young Tiberius and Gaius learned not only about the past heroes of Rome but also about how they could become heroes themselves.

Cornelia knew that Rome was filled with inequality; the rich were getting richer, and the poor were struggling. Her lessons often highlighted the need for change and reforms that would help everyone in Rome, not just the wealthy. These discussions around their dinner table ignited a fire in the hearts of the young brothers.

The Gracchi Brothers' Reforms

Inspired by their mother's teachings, Tiberius and Gaius grew up to propose revolutionary reforms. Tiberius, the elder, became a tribune and introduced laws to redistribute land to the poor. Gaius, following in his brother's footsteps, also became a tribune and pushed for laws that provided grain at reduced prices for the poor. He even suggested citizenship for all Italians, not just Romans.

Their efforts, though initially popular, faced fierce opposition from the elite classes. Yet, the courage and conviction that Cornelia had instilled in them drove the brothers to fight for their beliefs, reshaping Roman policies and stirring significant changes in the republic.

Revered for Her Virtues

Cornelia's influence was not limited to her immediate family. In Rome, she was revered as a model of Roman virtue. She was known for her intelligence, her eloquence, and her stoic grace, especially in the face of personal tragedy. Even after the tragic deaths of both her sons—who were assassinated because of their political reforms—Cornelia remained a pillar of strength.

Because of this reputation, people from all over both Rome and Italy would come to see her. She often spoke about the pride she felt in her sons' efforts to make Rome a better place for all its citizens rather than bitterness at their unexpected deaths.

Cornelia's Enduring Legacy

Today, Cornelia Scipionis Africana is remembered not just as the mother of the Gracchi brothers but as a symbol of maternal influence and civic duty. Her story teaches us that behind great leaders are often great teachers. In Cornelia's case, she taught her sons that true nobility comes not from one's heritage but from one's service to the community.

As you walk through the historical tales of Rome, remember Cornelia as an example of how one person's teachings can ignite the flame of change and inspire generations to come. Just like the stars that shine above the ruins of ancient Rome, Cornelia's virtues and wisdom continue to shine..

Cleopatra VII: The Queen Who Swayed Rome (51 - 30 BC)

Now we will jump to the ancient and mysterious land of Egypt, where a queen who had a mind as sharp as the point of a pyramid and a will as strong as the stones that built them lived. Her name was Cleopatra VII, and she was the last pharaoh of Egypt. Cleopatra was not just any queen; she also played a pivotal role in the history of both Egypt and Rome.

Cleopatra's Royal Alliances

Cleopatra came to power in a time of turmoil. She was both queen and diplomat. She knew that forming alliances was key to maintaining power and protecting her kingdom. Her most famous alliances were with two of the most powerful men in Rome: Julius Caesar and Mark Antony.

It was in Egypt, where the Nile River flowed and pyramids touched the sky, that Cleopatra first allied with the mighty Roman general, Julius Caesar. Caesar had come to Egypt chasing his rival, Pompey. In this coincidence, Cleopatra saw an opportunity. In a famous event, she was wrapped in a rug and delivered to Caesar. At her arrival, she unveiled herself as a queen who sought his support. With Caesar's help, she solidified her grip on the Egyptian throne.

After Caesar's tragic assassination, Cleopatra found another Roman ally in Mark Antony, a dashing and ambitious leader. Together, they dreamed of creating a new empire that would combine the strengths of Egypt and Rome. Their partnership was not only political but also romantic, and they had three children together.

Impact on History

Cleopatra's alliances with these powerful Roman figures were not just love stories; they were strategic moves that shaped the fates of Egypt and Rome. With Julius Caesar, Cleopatra hoped to stabilize her country and assert her power against her rivals. With Mark Antony, she aimed to further expand her influence, envisioning a world where her son could rule Rome and Egypt.

Unfortunately, Cleopatra's dreams would lead to dramatic and deadly results. Her involvement with Roman leaders plunged Egypt into the complex political struggles of Rome. When Mark Antony declared his loyalty to Cleopatra over Rome, it sparked a conflict with Octavian (the future Emperor Augustus), who saw Antony as a traitor influenced by a foreign queen. The rivalry turned into a great sea battle at Actium, where Octavian's forces defeated Antony and Cleopatra. This defeat marked the end of the Ptolemaic dynasty in Egypt and the beginning of Roman rule.

Cleopatra's Legacy

Cleopatra's life was a tapestry woven with ambition, romance, and tragedy. Her death—by a supposed snake bite—marked the end of an era in Egypt. However, her impact on history remains as enduring as the sands of her Egyptian desert.

Cleopatra is remembered not only as a beautiful and charismatic queen but also as a shrewd and capable ruler who navigated her kingdom through the treacherous waters of Roman politics. Her story teaches us about the power of intelligence and determination, showing that a queen can influence the rise and fall of empires.

As you reflect on the stories of powerful women in Roman history, remember Cleopatra as the queen who swayed Rome. Her tale reminds us that history is not just about battles and conquests, but also about the alliances and decisions that can shape the world.

Chapter Conclusion

We've explored the lives of some incredible women who played key roles in ancient Rome. Through their stories, we learned how women were able to navigate a world dominated by men, using their intelligence, courage, and determination to influence the course of history. From Livia's strategic thinking to Cornelia's nurturing yet firm guidance of her sons, these women showed that strength comes in many forms.

As we close this chapter, we carry with us the inspiring tales of these powerful women. Their contributions remind us that everyone has the potential to make a difference. Now, let's turn the page and continue our journey through ancient Rome, ready to uncover more fascinating aspects of this historic empire. Onto the next adventure!

CHAPTER 3:
BRAVE GLADIATORS OF THE COLOSSEUM

Now, it's time to step into the world of ancient Rome's most thrilling entertainers. In this chapter, we'll meet the fearless gladiators who battled in the grand Colosseum. These were not just fighters; they were real-life heroes to the people who watched them. From the swift and strategic Retiarii with their nets and tridents to the heavily-armored Murmillo, each gladiator had a unique style and a brave heart.

Get ready to discover what made these fighters tick, how they lived, and how they became the stars of the most spectacular shows in all of ancient Rome. Let's dive into the exciting and daring world of the gladiators!

TYPES OF GLADIATORS

In ancient Rome, the Colosseum roared with the cheers of spectators as gladiators clashed in epic battles. These warriors were not only skilled fighters but also masters of different combat styles, each with their unique weapons and tactics. Among them, the Retiarii, Secutores, Bestiarii, Murmillo, and Thraex stood out for their distinctive roles and thrilling performances. Let's dive into the fascinating world of these ancient superstars and explore what made each type of gladiator a favorite in the sands of the arena.

Retiarii: The Net Fighters of the Arena

Imagine going fishing, but instead of catching fish, you're trying to catch other gladiators in a big, sandy arena! That's what it was like to be a *Retiarius* (that's the singular form of *Retiarii*). These gladiators carried a trident, which is a long three-pronged spear. Many Tridents would have been similar to what you see the sea god Neptune. These gladiators also had a *rete*, or a net, which they used to entangle their opponents from a distance.

In addition to their net and trident, *Retiarii* wore minimal armor. They usually had a shoulder guard on their left side, called a *galerus*, which protected their head and neck from incoming blows. This light armor allowed them to move quickly and freely, which was crucial for their fighting technique.

Fighting Style and Strategy

The *Retiarii* were like the sneaky tricksters of the gladiator world. Their strategy was to keep their distance and use their net to snare their opponents. Once the enemy was tangled, the *Retiarius* would use his trident to strike. If the net missed or the opponent got free, the *Retiarius* had to rely on his speed and agility to dodge attacks and prepare for another chance to throw his net.

Retiarii typically fought against heavily armored gladiators like the *Secutores* or the *Murmillos*. These opponents carried big shields and swords but moved slower due to their heavy gear. The battles between the lightly equipped *Retiarii* and the heavily armored secutores were dramatic and full of suspense, showcasing a classic matchup of speed versus strength.

The Challenge of Being a *Retiarius*

Being a *Retiarius* was not easy. Their lighter armor meant they had less protection, making them vulnerable to strikes from their opponent's sword. This required the *Retiarius* to be very skillful and clever. They had to use their nets not just to entrap but also to protect themselves and to create opportunities for attack.

The crowd loved watching *Retiarii* because their fights were unpredictable and filled with clever tactics. A successful net throw could change the outcome of a match in an instant. Crowds would cheer wildly whenever a *Retiarius* managed to ensnare his heavily armored opponent.

Today, when we think about gladiators, we can imagine the *Retiarii* as the clever artists of the arena. They could turn what could have been a straightforward fight into a display of strategy and skill. Their legacy teaches us the value of quick thinking and adaptability, andshowing that that sometimes, being smart and swift is just as important as being strong.

Secutores: The Chasing Gladiators

Secutores, were known as the "chasers." These powerful gladiators were famous for their battles against the tricky *Retiarii*, who fought with nets and tridents. The games between *Secutores* and *Retiarii* were like a dramatic dance of cat and mouse, where strength and strategy clashed in exciting displays.

The Armor of the *Secutores*

Imagine dressing up in a suit of armor that's not just for show, but for protection in fierce battles! That was the life of a *Secutor*. Each piece of their gear was designed to help them succeed in their main job: catching and overcoming the swift *Retiarii*.

The Secutor's helmet was heavy and unique, and looked almost like a big metal bucket with only two small eye-holes. Though this design protected him from being hooked by a Retiarius's trident, it also made it hard to see. Their helmets were smooth with no sharp edges that a Retiarius's net could snag on. It was like wearing a big, metal bucket on your head, but much more carefully designed! They also carried a large rectangular shield, called a "scutum," which covered most of their body. This shield was their main defense against the Retiarius's trident and net. Along with the shield, they wore armor on their arms and legs, and a padded linen guard over their torso, making them look like knights ready for a battle.

The Life of a *Secutor*

Secutores had to be very strong and also quite clever. They carried heavy weapons and armor, which meant they needed to be powerful enough to move quickly and withstand long fights. Their main weapon was a short sword, called a "*gladius*," perfect for close combat once they managed to get past the swirling net of a *Retiarius*.

In the arena, the Secutores job was to chase down Retiarius, who would try to keep his distance and entangle Secutore from afar. This made fights between a Secutores and a Retiarius extremely suspenseful. The audience never knew if the Secutore would manage to shield himself from the net and close in on the Retiarius, or if he'd get caught and face the sharp point of the trident.

The Challenges and Strategies

Being a Secutore wasn't just about strength; it was also about smarts and strategy. They had to judge the right moment to advance and the right moment to hold back, all while carrying heavy gear and looking through tiny holes in a massive helmet. They also had to be patient, waiting for the Retiarius to make a mistake. When their opponent faltered, they had to act quickly. Not only did their bodies have to handle the weight, and the heat of the battle but also their minds to react to the cunning tactics of their opponents.

So, when you think of the *Secutores*, remember them as the brave gladiators who were "chasers' ' of the arena, always ready to face challenges head-on. They show us how determination and protection can lead to victory in the face of adversity. They were not just fighters; they were heroes of the Roman world, whose stories of bravery continue to inspire us today.

Bestiarii: The Wild Animal Fighters of Rome

The *Bestiarii* were also gladiators, but their role was unique. Instead of clashing swords with other warriors, they took on wild beasts like lions, bears, and even elephants. These fights were part of the broader spectacle of Roman games, which included chariot races, theatrical plays, and much more. The *Bestiarii*'s battles were a big draw for the public, offering a mix of danger and excitement.

Training and Gear

Becoming a *Bestiarius* was a serious choice as they only fought. These fighters trained specifically to handle wild animals. They had to move quickly, stay alert, and use their weapons effectively against unpredictable opponents. Their main tools were usually a spear or a short sword, designed to keep the animals at bay while delivering a decisive blow.

Unlike their fellow gladiators, *Bestiarii* often wore lighter armor. This allowed them more speed and agility, which were crucial in outmaneuvering large and dangerous animals. However, this also meant they were less protected, making their role both spectacular and incredibly risky.

The Day of the Battle

On the day of the games, the atmosphere in the Colosseum would be electric. Spectators from all walks of life, from the wealthiest senators to the common folk, filled the stands. They were all eager to watch the *Bestiarii* in action. The arena floor would be transformed for these fights, sometimes filled with elaborate scenery to mimic the natural habitats of the animals being fought.

When the *Bestiarius* entered the arena, the crowd would erupt in cheers. Then, the gates would open, and the wild animals would be released. Imagine the tension in the air as a Bestiarius stood alone, spear in hand, facing down a roaring lion. Each movement had to be calculated and precise—; a single mistake could be fatal.

The Challenges They Faced

The life of a *Bestiarius* was filled with constant danger. Like the *Secutores* and *Retiarii,* These gladiators had to be both physically strong and mentally sharp. But, they also needed to understand the behaviors of different animals and use this knowledge to survive. Their fights were not just brute force; they were moments of intense strategy and daring.

Despite the risks, being a *Bestiarius* brought fame and admiration. Successful *Bestiarii* were celebrated as the heroes who were able to conquer nature itself. Their victories were a testament to human bravery and skill, themes loved by the Roman public.

Murmillo: The Heavily- Armored Gladiator

The *Murmillo* gladiators were imposing figures in the arena, equipped with a large shield and a *gladius* (the same short sword used by *Secutores)* known as a gladius. Their helmet was distinctively large and often featured a fish-like crest on top. – Unsurprisingly, "*murmillo*" comes from the Greek word for a type of fish, hinting at the shape of their helmets. This unique gear not only provided excellent protection but also added to their intimidating presence.

The Armor and Weapons

Imagine wearing the armor of a *Murmillo*—going into a battle wearing a heavy helmet that covers your whole head, a large rectangular shield that protects most of your body, and carrying a sharp sword to defend you. This was the daily uniform of a Murmillo. Their armor was designed to offer maximum protection during fights, making them look like walking fortresses.

The *Murmillo*'s shield was called a *scutum*. It was their primary defense tool., It was used to block attacks from opponents and counterattack when an opportunity presented itself. Like other gladiators, the *gladius*, a deadly short sword, was their main offensive weapon, ideal for close combat and powerful, precise strikes.

Training and Life in the *Ludus*

Becoming a *Murmillo* required rigorous training. These gladiators spent countless hours practicing with their weapons, strengthening their bodies to carry heavy armor, and learning tactics to best opponents with different fighting styles. Life in the *ludus* (which was what they called gladiator school) was strict and disciplined, with every day centered around enhancing physical strength and combat skills.

Young readers might find it interesting to know that despite their fearsome appearances in the arena, many *Murmillo* gladiators formed friendships with their fellow fighters and even with their trainers. The bond formed in the *ludus* was strong, as they relied on each other for survival and success.

The Legacy of the *Murmillo*

The *Murmillo* were not just fighters; they were a symbol of strength and endurance. Their battles in the arenas of ancient Rome left a lasting impression on the public, both for the ferocity of their fighting style and the resilience they displayed against different types of gladiators.

As you think about the Murmillo, imagine them as the ancient superheroes of the arena., Theirtheir battles are a testament to the human spirit's capability to strive for victory in the face of overwhelming odds. Their story is not just one of combat but of the enduring human desire to excel and triumph.

Thraex: The Swift Warriors of the Arena

The *Thraex* gladiators were dressed to resemble the warriors of Thrace, famous for their courage and fighting prowess. In the grand arenas of Rome, these gladiators captivated crowds with their exotic weapons and swift movements, offering a glimpse into the warrior culture of Thrace.

Gear and Weapons of the *Thraex*

Imagine stepping into an arena with a small, square shield and a curved sword. This was the typical gear of a *Thraex* including a small, square shield and a curved sword. Their shield, called a *parma*, was much smaller than the large rectangular *scutum* used by many other gladiators. *Parmas* allowed for quicker, more agile movements so the *Thraex* could. The shield was designed to protect themselves while also enabling swift offensive maneuvers, reactive combat maneuvers.

Fighting Style and Strategy

The *Thraex* gladiators had to use their speed and agility to compensate for their smaller shields and lack of heavy armor. They were trained to be quick on their feet, using their agility to dodge blows and to position themselves advantageously against slower, more heavily armored opponents.

Training and Life as a *Thraex*

Becoming a *Thraex* required intense training. These gladiators spent hours each day honing their skills with the *sica*, learning how to make the most of their weapon's unique shape. They practiced maneuvers to dart in and strike quickly before slipping away from an enemy's counterattack, much like modern fencing athletes.

The Legacy of the *Thraex*

The *Thraex* gladiators brought a distinct flavor to the Roman games, showcasing the art of Thracian warfare. Their battles demonstrated that in the arena, as in life, being adaptable and quick-thinking often leads to success. The sight of a Thraex, darting with his curved sword, became a symbol of agility and cunning in combat. Imagine them as the agile dancers of the arena, their battles a thrilling spectacle dance of swords and shields. They show us that even in the toughest situations, using one's unique strengths creatively can pave the way to victory.

LEGENDARY GLADIATORS

Spartacus: The Gladiator Who Fought for Freedom

Let's begin in the Roman Republic with Spartacus—one of the most legendary heroes of ancient times. Spartacus was not just any gladiator; rather, he was a leader who dared to challenge the vast and powerful city of Rome in a fight for freedom. His story is one of courage, strength, and the unyielding desire for liberty.

Spartacus was originally from Thrace, a place near modern-day Bulgaria. Thrace was not part of Rome, but it did have its own wild and fierce history. Spartacus was a strong man who was skilled with weapons that was ultimately captured by Roman soldiers. Instead of working quietly as a slave, Spartacus was trained to be a gladiator—a fighter who entertained crowds by battling other gladiators or wild animals in large arenas (like the Colosseum).

Imagine being taken to a strange land and forced to fight for your life for the amusement of others. That was the harsh world Spartacus lived in. But he had a heart filled with hope and a mind sharp as a sword. Spartacus was more than a fighter; he was a thinker and a dreamer. His dream was to achieve freedom for himself and his fellow slaves.

The Great Escape

Spartacus's desire for freedom eventually turned into action. Along with about 70 fellow gladiators, he orchestrated a daring escape from a gladiator school in Capua. Using nothing more than kitchen utensils to start the rebellion, the gladiators fought their way out, capturing real weapons from their defeated guards along the way.

Once free, Spartacus and his band of gladiators found refuge on the slopes of Mount Vesuvius. There, they set up camp and planned their next moves. Spartacus's bravery and wisdom quickly made him the leader of the group. He knew that staying free would be even harder than breaking free.

But Spartacus was ready to face whatever challenges came his way.

The Third Servile War

What started as a small group of escaped gladiators soon became a massive army. As word spread of Spartacus and his fight against Rome, thousands of slaves joined him, growing his army to over 70,000 members. These were not just men who wanted to fight; they were people who craved freedom, who wanted to return to their homes, and who no longer wished to live under the harsh rule of their masters.

Spartacus's army of freed slaves won several battles against Roman forces, which was a big embarrassment for Rome. Imagine the most powerful empire in the world being challenged by a group led by a former gladiator! Spartacus and his followers were soon seen as heroes to some and dangerous rebels to others.

The Legacy of Spartacus

The story of Spartacus does not have a happy ending. After two years of fighting, the Roman army finally defeated Spartacus's forces. Historians believe that Spartacus himself fell in battle and his body was never found. However, the spirit of Spartacus could not be defeated. He became a symbol of hope and resistance for all those oppressed. His story has been told and retold in many ways—through books, movies, and songs—each celebrating his strength and his struggle for freedom.

Remember Spartacus not just as a gladiator who fought wild beasts for entertainment but as a hero who fought for a much greater cause of freedom. His courage reminds us that even in the face of overwhelming odds, fighting for what is right is the bravest battle of all.

Crixus: The Gladiator Who Dreamed of Freedom

Among the mighty gladiators that clashed in the grand arenas of ancient Rome, Spartacus was not the only warrior whose heart beat with the fierce rhythm of freedom. There was another gladiator named Crixus, which meant "one with curly hair" in his native language, Gaulish. Crixus was not just any gladiator—he was a leader in one of the biggest slave revolts in Roman history, the Third Servile War.

From Gaul to Gladiator

Crixus was born in Gaul, a vast area covering modern France and parts of its neighboring countries. As a young man, he was captured by Roman forces, taken from his homeland, and sold into slavery. Though the details of his capture are a mystery, his destiny was to become one of the most famous gladiators in Rome.

Imagine being taken from your home and forced to fight for the entertainment of those who captured you. That was the life Crixus was thrown into. He trained in the gladiator school of Capua, where he learned to fight. His education taught him not just to survive, but to excel. Crixus became a powerful warrior, skilled with various weapons and the art of combat.

The Spark of Revolt

Despite his fame in the arena, Crixus's heart longed for freedom. He found a kindred spirit in Spartacus, as both were determined to break the chains of slavery. Together with Spartacus and a small group of other gladiators, Crixus made a bold escape from the gladiator school.

Once free, Crixus and Spartacus gathered other slaves and disenchanted souls, forming an army that would challenge the very foundation of Rome. Crixus was not only a fierce warrior, but also a charismatic leader. He inspired his followers with dreams of returning to their homes and escaping the tyranny of their masters.

As their numbers grew, the rebels, led by Spartacus and Crixus, won several battles against Roman forces. Crixus's bravery and fighting skills were crucial to these victories. He fought with a passion that ignited courage in the hearts of his comrades. However, as the war progressed, differences in strategy began to emerge between Spartacus and Crixus. Spartacus wanted to escape over the Alps, believing that dispersing their forces would keep them safe from Roman retaliation. Crixus, however, wanted to strike directly at Rome until every slave in Italy was free.

The Legend of Crixus

Eventually, Spartacus and Crixus differences caused them to split, each with part of the army. Crixius continued to harass Roman forces, achieving great feats on the battlefield. But, the divided army would eventually lead to Crixus's downfall. In a fierce battle near Mount Gargano, Crixus and his followers faced a large Roman army. Despite their bravery, Crixus and many of his warriors were killed, marking a tragic end to his quest for freedom.

Crixus's life was a testament to the spirit of resistance. He may not have successfully freed all of the slaves in the empire, but his actions left a mark on history. His courage and determination in the face of overwhelming odds inspired not only his contemporaries but generations to come.

Today, when we think of gladiators, we often picture them fighting in the arena. But Crixus reminds us that some gladiators fought for something greater: their freedom. His story teaches us about the power of hope and the unbreakable human spirit that can thrive even in the darkest of times.

Flamma: The Gladiator Who Chose the Arena

While the once-gladiators Crixus and Spartacus stood out due to their fight for freedom, another gladiator was notable for his dedication to stay in the arena even when the gates of freedom were opened to him. His name was Flamma, which means "flame" in Latin. And, true to his name, Flamma was a fiery and fierce warrior who captured the hearts of many.

Flamma came from Syria, a land rich with history and culture, and far from the bustling streets of Rome. As a young man, he was captured and brought to Rome, where he was trained to be a gladiator. This was a tough life, filled with danger at every turn, but Flamma excelled in the art of combat.

Gladiators like Flamma fought in grand arenas like the famous Colosseum. Here, battling against other gladiators, wild animals, and sometimes staged reenactments of famous battles, gladiators gained honor and recognition, even though they were slaves.

A Champion in the Arena

Flamma was a powerhouse in the arena. He fought 34 battles, winning 21 of them. With each victory, his fame grew. He soon became a favorite among the Roman spectators. Gladiators who performed well in the arena were sometimes rewarded with a *rudis*—or, a wooden sword that symbolized their freedom. It was the ultimate prize for a gladiator, a ticket to a new life away from the deadly sands of the arena.

However, Flamma was no ordinary gladiator. He was offered the *rudis* not just once, but four times throughout his career. Each time, he rejected this offer of freedom. Flamma's decision to stay a gladiator baffled many, but to him, the arena was where he felt most alive. The thrill of the fight, the cheers of the crowd, and the glory of victory were what he cherished most.

Why Stay a Gladiator?

You might wonder, why would someone choose the dangerous life of a gladiator over freedom? For Flamma, the reasons could be many. Perhaps he felt a sense of belonging in the arena, a place where he was respected and admired rather than just another slave. Or maybe he loved the thrill of competition and the camaraderie with other gladiators, sharing a bond forged in the heat of battle.

Being a star in the arena also gave Flamma a sense of purpose and achievement. He knew the risks, but he also knew the glory. Every time he stepped into the Colosseum, he wasn't just fighting for survival; he was fighting to be remembered, to leave a legacy that would outlive him.

Flamma's choice to remain a gladiator made him a legend. He showed that sometimes, we find our true calling in the most unexpected places. For Flamma, the arena was his home, and ultimately the gladiator's life was his chosen path. Today, Flamma is remembered not just for his victories in the arena, but for his courage to follow his heart. His story teaches us about the values of determination, bravery, and the pursuit of what makes us truly happy, even if that choice is unexpected.

Tetraites: The Hero of the Arena

Flamma was not the only gladiator who was extremely skilled in the Colosseum. Another famous gladiator, Tetraites, became a legendary fighter as well. He was a *murmillo*, or a type of gladiator known for wearing a large helmet with a fish-like crest on top and also carrying a big shield and sword. But Tetraites wasn't just a fighter; rather, he was also a symbol of bravery and skill who captured the imagination of all who saw him battle.

A Star in Roman Culture

Tetraites's popularity went beyond the arena. His exploits were talked about in the streets, written about in poems, and even painted as graffiti on the walls of Rome. People admired his strength and prowess, and he soon became a part of Roman pop culture, much like movie stars today.

Artifacts from that time, like small figurines and mosaics, are proof of just how admired he was. These items often depicted Tetraites in his *murmillo* armor after a victory. People in Rome might have kept these as souvenirs, much like we might keep posters or action figures of our favorite heroes today.

Being a star gladiator like Tetraites was a strange mix of fame and danger. On the one hand, Tetraites enjoyed fame and the adoration of fans. On the other hand, every time he stepped into the arena, he faced real danger. Gladiators often fought to the death, and even though many battles ended with mercy—when the defeated gladiator was spared—every fight could have been his last.

This mix of danger and fame made Tetraites's life exciting but also very challenging. He had to maintain his strength and skills, always preparing for the next battle, knowing that his survival depended not just on his ability to fight but also on his ability to win over the crowd.

Tetraites's Legacy

Tetraites's impact on Roman culture shows us how sports and entertainment have always been important. Just like modern sports stars, gladiators brought excitement and drama into people's lives, giving them heroes to cheer for and stories to tell.

Tetraites's legacy teaches us about how the love for stories of struggle and triumph is a part of the human experience. He remains a symbol of the timeless appeal of heroes and the games that showcase their courage still today.

Priscus and Verus: The Gladiator Brothers

Though gladiators like Tetraites often became legendary due to their skill in the arena alone, two warriors defied this stereotype. They were Priscus and Verus, two gladiators who were not brothers by birth, but became brothers in battle. They shared one of the most famous fights in the history of the gladiators.

Priscus and Verus were both originally slaves, captured in wars and brought to Rome to train as gladiators. Gladiators like Priscus and Verus trained for months, learning how to fight with various weapons, how to protect themselves, and how to entertain a crowd. Their lives were tough, but they knew that if they could win the favor of the public, they might earn their freedom with the *rudis*.

The Battle of Equals

The day that Priscus and Verus stepped into the Colosseum to face each other was a day of celebration in Rome. It was the 100th day of games commissioned by the Emperor Titus to inaugurate the opening of the Colosseum, and the city was alive with excitement. People from all over the empire came to watch, eager to see the grand battles.

During these special games, Priscus and Verus faced off. They were well-matched in skill and courage. So, as they fought, it became clear that this was no ordinary match. They exchanged blow for blow, their swords clashing, shields banging, and the crowd roaring with each move. The battle was long and fierce, and neither warrior could gain the upper hand.

As the fight wore on, both gladiators grew tired, but neither would yield. Their respect for each other grew with every pass of their swords, and so did the crowd's respect for them. The fight seemed to last forever, and the spectators were held spellbound by the spectacle of these two incredible warriors. Priscus and Verus fought not just for their lives but for honor and freedom.

Finally, both gladiators were too exhausted to continue, and the battle was declared a draw. This was a rare occurrence in the gladiatorial games, where usually only one gladiator could be victorious. The crowd, moved by the bravery and endurance of both men, erupted in cheers, calling for their freedom. The emperor, impressed by their skill and spirit, granted both Priscus and Verus their freedom. They were awarded the *rudis*, (the same symbolic wooden sword that Flamma denied many times) which freed them both from their service as gladiators. The poet Martial, who witnessed the fight, wrote about it to celebrate their courage and the historic nature of their battle.

Heroes of the Arena

The story of Priscus and Verus is more than just a tale of a fight; it's a story about determination, skill, and mutual respect. These two men proved that they were not just entertainers—rather, they were warriors of the highest order. Their battle showed that even in the harsh world of the gladiators, there was room for honor and brotherhood.

Today, Priscus and Verus are remembered not only for their epic battle, but also as proof that even in the face of great challenges, friendship and respect can prevail.

Chapter Conclusion

Now we've journeyed alongside many Roman heroes, including the brave gladiators of ancient Rome. We explored their fierce battles and learned about the lives they led both in and out of the Colosseum. These gladiators were more than just fighters; they were symbols of bravery and skill, capturing the imaginations of thousands of spectators who watched them perform in the arena.

As we close this chapter, we reflect on the incredible courage these individuals displayed, facing formidable foes and dangerous beasts for the entertainment of others. Their legacy teaches us about the Roman values of strength and honor, and their stories continue to fascinate us today.

CHAPTER 4:
MIGHTY GODS & GODDESSES OF ROME

In this chapter, we're going to meet the amazing gods and goddesses that the ancient Romans believed in and worshiped. From Jupiter, the powerful king of the gods, to Juno, the queen who watched over all marriages, each deity had their own special powers and exciting stories. Get ready to explore the magical myths and fascinating roles these celestial characters played in the daily lives of the Romans. Welcome to a new adventure full of mighty deeds and divine wonders!

Saturn: The God of Time and Renewal

In the ancient Roman pantheon, where gods held dominion over everything from the depths of the sea to the expanse of the sky, Saturn reigned over some of the most fundamental aspects of life and the universe. Known as the god of time, agriculture, wealth, and renewal, Saturn was a complex deity whose influence touched the lives of all Romans, from farmers tilling the fields to citizens celebrating the new year.

Saturn was often depicted as a wise old man holding a sickle, which he used to harvest crops but also symbolized his connection to the cycles of creation and dissolution. This tool highlighted his dual role as a god of both agriculture and time.

The Role of Saturn in Roman Mythology

Saturn's mythology is rich with stories of power, loss, and revival. According to legend, Saturn was once the king of the gods., He ruleding during a golden age of prosperity and peace. During his reign, there was abundance and joy, and the earth provided without the need for extra worktoil. However, Saturn was overthrown by his son Jupiter.

Though he was conqueredDespite his overthrow, Saturn's spirit of abundance and liberation lived on. He was celebrated as a liberator, freeing those bound by time and fate. His return at the end of each year during the festival of *Saturnalia* brought a temporary return to the golden age he once ruled over.

Saturnalia: The Festival of Saturn

The festival of *Saturnalia* was one of the most important and joyous events in the Roman calendar. It was hHeld in December, during the winter solstice, it celebrated the return of the golden age. For a week, social norms were turned upside down;: slaves were served by their masters, all work and business were suspended, and the streets filled with merry celebrations.

Families exchanged gifts such as, especially wax candles. These candles signified the light returning after the solstice, symbolizing the hope and the rebirth of life that comes with the new agricultural year. *Saturnalia* showcased Saturn's roles as the god of time, renewal, and liberation from the usual social and physical constraints.

Saturn's Legacy

Today, Saturn's name lives on in the planet Saturn, known for its beautiful rings that circle endlessly, much like the cycles of time he governed. His legacy also continues in the celebration of *Saturnalia*., which This festival has influenced modern holiday traditions, such as Christmas and the New Year.

As you think about Saturn, remember him as a god who reminds us of the importance of time, the joy of renewal, and the value of freedom.

Jupiter: The King of Roman Gods

Imagine a grand figure, towering with strength, wearing a robe that sparkles like the stars, and holding a lightning bolt as fierce as his gaze. This is Jupiter, the supreme deity of the Roman pantheon. His role was to oversee all aspects of life and rule over the other gods, making sure that peace and order prevailed.

Maybe you know Jupiter by his Greek name, Zeus. Since the Romans gave him his own distinct personality and stories, the name Jupiter is just as important. He was the god of the sky, which meant he controlled the weather (especially thunderstorms and lightning). These served as his weapons to show his displeasure or to fight against those who crossed him.

Jupiter's Family and Friends

Jupiter was part of a divine family that ruled the skies and the Earth. He was the son of Saturn, the god of time, and Ops, the goddess of wealth. Jupiter's brothers and sisters included Neptune, the god of the sea, and Pluto, the god of the underworld.

Jupiter was married to Juno, the goddess of marriage and childbirth, who was also his sister. Together, they lived on Mount Olympus, the mythical home of the gods, which was said to be perched high above the clouds, unreachable by mere mortals.

Jupiter, the Protector of Rome

Jupiter was not only a powerful god but also a champion of the Roman people. The Romans believed that Jupiter watched over their city and protected its people from harm, whether from natural disasters or enemy attacks. This made him an extremely important figure in Roman religion.

The worship of Jupiter was at the heart of Roman religious life. The largest temple in Rome, the magnificent Temple of Jupiter Optimus Maximus, was dedicated to him. It stood on Capitoline Hill, one of the seven hills of Rome. The temple served as a place where Romans offered prayers and sacrifices, hoping to gain Jupiter's favor.

Stories and Myths Involving Jupiter

Jupiter was central to many Roman myths and stories, which often involved his adventures, his battles to maintain order, and his relationships with other gods and mortals. One famous myth is how he became the King of Gods; in this myth, Jupiter led his siblings in a rebellion against their tyrannical father, Saturn, the ancient god of time. Jupiter was able to overthrow Saturn and then divide the universe among his brothers.

Another popular story tells of Jupiter's defeat of the giant Typhon, a terrifying creature that threatened all gods and humans. Using his mighty lightning bolts, Jupiter battled Typhon. After a fierce fight, Jupiter trapped the giant under Mount Etna. This story was a favorite among Roman children, much like superhero tales are today!

Jupiter's Legacy

Jupiter's influence was seen everywhere in Roman culture, such as in public festivals like the spectacular Games of Jupiter. These events featured athletic competitions, chariot races, and theatrical performances, all held in his honor. Today, when we look up at the vast sky or watch a storm, we can remember Jupiter, the Roman King of Gods. His stories of bravery, leadership, and protection remind us of the values the Romans held dear—strength, justice, and the care for the community.

Juno: The Queen of Roman Gods

High above the busy streets of ancient Rome, in the mystical realm of the gods, reigned Juno, the revered Queen of the Gods. Juno, who had a majestic presence and offered wise counsel, was not just any goddess—she was the protector of the Roman state and the divine symbol of marriage and childbirth.

Imagine a powerful and graceful queen, draped in beautiful robes, her eyes filled with wisdom and care. This is Juno, the daughter of Saturn. Juno was also the sister and wife of mighty king Jupiter. As the queen of the gods, Juno held a special place in the hearts of the Roman people. She was revered not only as a goddess of marriage but also as a guardian of the Roman state, offering protection and advice to her followers.

Juno, the Goddess of Marriage

Juno's role as the goddess of marriage was central to her identity. She watched over married couples and families, blessing marriages with happiness and prosperity. The

Romans believed that Juno's favor was crucial for a harmonious family life.Many would offer prayers and sacrifices to her on their wedding day, hoping to receive her blessings.

Every year, Roman women celebrated the festival of *Matronalia* in honor of Juno. This special day was dedicated to happiness and well-being in married life. Wives received gifts from their husbands, and prayers were offered to Juno asking for strong, loving relationships. It was a day filled with joy and festivities, reflecting Juno's importance in the lives of Roman families.

Juno, the Protector of the State

Juno's role, however, extended beyond personal and family life; she was also the protector and counselor of the Roman state. This responsibility was a vital aspect of her divine duties. The Romans believed that Juno watched over their city, safeguarding its people and its leaders. Leaders and soldiers alike would seek her guidance and protection before making important decisions or going into battle.

The Temple of Juno, *Moneta*, located on the Capitoline Hill alongside the Temple of Jupiter, was a testament to her importance. *Moneta* comes from the Latin word for "warn" or "advise," which reflects Juno's role as an advisor. Interestingly, her temple was not just a religious site, but also the place where Rome's mint was located. This was symbolic of Juno's protective watch over the city's wealth and well-being.

Myths and Stories Involving Juno

Juno appears in many myths and stories. In these stories, she often shows her protective nature, but sometimes her jealousy and rivalry with other gods and mortals who crossed her or her loved ones came out. Despite these challenges, Juno was always respected by the other gods and goddesses, and her wisdom was unmatched.

One famous story involves Juno's peacock. According to legend, Juno transformed Argus, her hundred-eyed servant, into a peacock. Argus's many eyes were transformed into the bird's stunning feathers. This story highlighted her ability to watch over many things at once, always keeping a close eye on the affairs of gods and humans.

Juno's Legacy

Today, when we think of Juno, we remember her legacy as one of nurturing care and wise counsel. These qualities made her a beloved figure in Roman mythology. As you explore the tales of the Roman gods and goddesses, think of Juno not just as a figure of power, but also as a beacon of protection and wisdom. Her stories teach us the importance of how we should care for others and guide them with wisdom, just as she did for the ancient Romans from her high throne in the heavens.

Neptune: The Mighty God of the Sea

Deep beneath the sparkling waters of the Mediterranean, past the rolling waves and the ocean's blue mysteries, lived Neptune, the Roman god of the sea. With his powerful trident in hand, Neptune ruled over all the waters of the world—from the tiniest freshwater stream to the vast and stormy Atlantic Ocean.

Neptune was one of the most powerful gods of Roman mythology, known for his command over water in all its forms. He was the brother of Jupiter, the king of the gods, and Pluto, the god of the Underworld. Together, these three brothers ruled the heavens, the Earth, and the Underworld, maintaining balance in the world.

The Worship of Neptune

All Romans had deep respect for Neptune, especially those whose lives were closely tied to the sea. Sailors and fishermen prayed to Neptune for safe voyages, especially before embarking on long and perilous journeys. Temples dedicated to Neptune were often located near the coast. During his festivals, Romans celebrated him with games, horse races, and offerings thrown into the sea as a tribute to his power.

One of the biggest celebrations in honor of Neptune was the *Neptunalia*, held during the heat of summer. People would build temporary shelters from branches, where they then feasted and drank spring water and wine to cool down. They thanked Neptune for providing relief from the summer heat.

Neptune in Mythology

In mythology, Neptun's mood could change quickly. He was quick to anger but also capable of great kindness. When Neptune was calm, the seas were peaceful and the sailors safe. But when he was angry, the oceans would churn and waves would crash fiercely against the shores, reflecting his stormy moods.

Like Juno and Jupiter, Neptune was also part of many famous mythological stories. He often appeared as a mediator in disputes among gods or as a formidable opponent to those who dared to challenge him. Much like his brother Jupiter as well, Neptune's romantic escapades were legendary and involved various nymphs and goddesses.

Neptune's Legacy

Today, Neptune's image is still very much alive in both art and literature. He represents the majesty and mystery of the ocean—a world that is beautiful and bountiful, yet fierce and unforgiving. He teaches us about the power of nature and the need to respect the seas and all bodies of water on our planet.

As you think about Neptune, imagine the vast blue seas, where rhythmic waves are controlled by the trident of a mighty god. He serves as a reminder to us of the ancient Romans' deep respect for the powers that govern the natural elements. Additionally, Neptune's stories encourage us to be just as mindful today of the natural world's strength and beauty.

Mars: The Mighty God of War and Agriculture

Mars was the son of Jupiter and Juno, the king and queen of the gods. With such powerful parents, Mars was bound to be a significant figure among the gods. Though many know him as a god of battle, he was more than that. Mars was also integral to agricultural success. These two aspects of his power made Mars immensely important to the Romans—both in their survival and in their conquests.

In war, Mars was the emblem of strength and bravery. He was often depicted in shimmering armor, ready to lead soldiers into battle. In times of peace, he was a symbol of fertility and growth, showing a softer side that brought life to crops and prosperity to the Roman people.

Mars and the Protection of Rome

Mars held a special place in the hearts of the Romans because he was seen as the protector of Rome itself. He watched over the city's military and its borders, ensuring that peace prevailed. His presence was invoked during various festivals and rituals, especially before embarking on military campaigns.

One of Mars's most famous legacies was fathering Romulus and Remus, the legendary founders of Rome. According to myth, Mars fell in love with a Vestal Virgin named Rhea Silvia, who gave birth to the twins. The twins were raised by a she-wolf and eventually established the city of Rome. Mars's involvement in the story of Romulus and Remus underscored his integral role in the foundation of the city.

Celebrations in Honor of Mars

Mars was celebrated throughout the Roman calendar, but his most prominent festivals were held in March (named after him) and October. These festivities marked the beginning and end of the military campaign season. The festivals were filled with ceremonies that included parades of soldiers, offerings of the first fruits of harvest, and prayers for successful farming and safekeeping of the troops.

The month of March began with the Festival of Mars, known as *Martius*. During *Martius,* the *Salii*, or dancing priests of Mars, moved through the city carrying sacred shields and singing hymns to invoke the god's protection and blessings. It was a vibrant and robust start to the year, filled with the promise of protection and bounty.

Mars in Roman Culture

Mars was more than a deity to the Romans; he was a central figure in their cultural identity. His dual role as a god of both war and agriculture reflected the Romans' values of courage and productivity. Like Mars, they Romans saw themselves as a strong people, capable of defending their republic and making the land fruitful.

Statues and images of Mars were common in Roman homes. These representations of Mars served not just as decorations, but also as symbols of safety and assurance. His temples were also places of refuge and strength, drawing people who sought the god's intervention in their lives.

Mars's Legacy

Today, Mars continues to be a symbol of "martial" prowess and defense. His name lives on in our word, "martial," which relates to war and military life. Even the planet Mars that glows in our night sky is named after this god because of its blood-red color. The planet Mars helps remind us of the god of war's enduring presence.

Venus: The Goddess of Love and Beauty

Imagine a goddess so beautiful she made flowers spring up wherever she walked, and everyone around her smiled. This is how one could imagine Venus, the Roman goddess whose very presence brought joy and love. In Roman myths, Venus was not only the goddess of romantic love, but also a symbol of fertility and the beauty of nature and humans alike.

Venus's influence was seen in gardens bursting with life, love that united couples, and any art form that celebrated beauty. Her powers were so vast that the Romans believed they affected everything from personal relationships to the growth of crops in the fields.

Venus and Her Famous Myths

Venus was central to many stories and myths that often involved romance and its struggles, as well as adventure. One of the most famous tales featuring Venus describes her relationship with Mars, the god of war. As they were opposites in every way—Venus, the emblem of love and beauty, and Mars, the symbol of war and aggression—their story highlights how love can unite the most unlikely characters.

Another beloved myth involves Venus's role in the tale of Aeneas. Aeneas was a Trojan hero who survived the Trojan War. He then traveled to Italy, where he became one of the ancestors of the Romans. Venus, as Aeneas's mother, guided and protected him throughout his journeys, showcasing her role not just as a goddess of beauty but as a mother and protector.

Celebrations in Honor of Venus

The Romans had a lot of respect for Venus. As such, they celebrated her through various festivals and rites. One particularly important celebration was the *Veneralia*. On this day, women would seek Venus's assistance in their love lives and marriages, praying for happiness and fidelity.

Temples dedicated to Venus were decorated with the finest flowers and artworks, turning them into places of incredible beauty that mirrored the goddess's attributes. Romans would visit these temples to pay tribute to Venus and ask for her blessings in their romantic endeavors and family life.

Venus in Roman Culture

Venus's impact on Roman culture was profound. She was often depicted in sculptures and paintings, which emphasized her attributes of ideal feminine beauty and grace. These artworks not only served as religious icons but also as cultural symbols of what were considered the greatest aesthetic and moral qualities.

Furthermore, Venus was a patron of the arts. Many believed she inspired artists, poets, and musicians to create works that celebrated love and beauty. Her influence even spread to Roman fashion, jewelry, and even personal grooming.

Venus's Legacy

Today, Venus is still synonymous with beauty and love. Her legacy survives in the arts, literature, and the names of flowers and other natural wonders (like the Venus flytrap). The planet Venus, shining bright and beautiful in the night sky, is also named after her. It serves as a testament to her enduring presence as a symbol of allure and splendor.

As you think about Venus, remember her not only as the goddess of love but as a symbol of the beauty in the world and in ourselves. Her stories teach us about the power of love and the cultivation of beauty in all its forms—whether in nature, relationships, or the arts.

Vulcan: The God of Fire and the Forge

Imagine a god with a strong, muscular figure, covered in soot from his forge (a place where blacksmiths create weapons and armor), working tirelessly by the glow of molten metal. This was how one could imagine Vulcan. He was a god whose skilled hands could craft anything from thunderbolts for Jupiter to armor for heroes and gods. Though he was another one of Jupiter and Juno's sons, he was quite different from his celestial siblings. Vulcan preferred the heat of his forge over the enchanting Mount Olympus.

Vulcan's Realm and Powers

Legend has it that Vulcan's workshop was located underneath Mount Etna in Sicily. Mount Etna is a real volcano whose eruptions were said to be caused by Vulcan working in his forge. Here, amid rivers of lava and fiery pits, Vulcan crafted masterpieces. He created everything from weapons that could win wars to delicate jewelry that could win hearts.

As the god of fire, Vulcan's role extended beyond mere craftsmanship. He was also associated with the destructive and renewing power of fire. In agriculture, he was seen as a figure who could prevent fires from damaging crops. On the other hand, in city life, people prayed to Vulcan for protection against accidental fires.

The Festivals of Vulcan

Vulcan was honored by the Romans during the *Vulcanalia*, a festival celebrated on August 23rd each year. On this day, Romans would hang their clothes and fabrics out in the sun, hoping that Vulcan would prevent these goods from catching fire throughout the year. It was a day to respect the power of fire. The festival served as a reminder of not only how dangerous fire could be, but also how necessary it was for Roman civilization.

Vulcan in Mythology

The mythology behind Vulcan's character and history is filled with themes of resilience and transformation. According to myth, he was born weak. This deformity caused Juno to cast him out of heaven. He fell for a whole day and night, eventually landing in the sea where he was raised by sea nymphs. This tough beginning gave Vulcan a uniquely sympathetic perspective among the gods, as he treasured underdogs and hard workers.

Vulcan went on to marry Venus This was an odd match, but symbolized the union of very different forces—fire and beauty with craftsmanship and grace.

Vulcan's Legacy

Today, Vulcan still symbolizes the art of smithing and metalworking. He is often thought of as the patron of various modern crafts that involve fire, such as welding and firefighting.

Vulcan teaches us the importance of using our skills to create and protect. His legacy reminds us that even the most humble craftsman can achieve greatness through hard work and dedication.

Mercury: The Swift Messenger God

Among the many fascinating Roman gods and goddesses came Mercury, who zipped through the skies as the quickest of the gods. He was also the most clever of all. Known as the messenger of the gods, Mercury carried news and commands throughout the heavens and to the world below. But his talents didn't stop there—Mercury was also the god of translators and interpreters, making him a key figure in the communication between gods and mortals.

Imagine a young god wearing winged sandals and a winged hat, darting through the skies with the speed of light. This was how many depicted Mercury (aka Hermes for the Greeks), the son of Jupiter and Maia, a Pleiades nymph and daughter of Atlas. With his quick wit and ability to move between worlds, Mercury was indispensable to the other gods.

The Role of Mercury

Mercury had several important jobs among the gods. His primary role was to deliver important messages between the gods, or from the gods to humans. This wasn't an easy job, considering it involved traveling great distances and often carrying secrets of great importance.

But Mercury's role extended beyond just carrying messages. As the god of translators and interpreters, he helped bridge the gap between different languages and cultures. This job was crucial while the Roman Empire was expanding and encompassing many different peoples. Mercury enabled understanding and unity through translation, helping to maintain peace and order.

Mercury and His Cleverness

Mercury was celebrated not only for his speed but also for his mind. He was known for his shrewdness and ability to solve problems that stumped others. One famous myth tells the story of how Mercury invented the lyre. As a newborn, he stole cattle from Apollo. Since Apollo was not happy about this, Mercury had to make amends. So, he crafted the lyre from a tortoise shell and gave it to Apollo, charming the sun god and earning his forgiveness.

Mercury also showed his cleverness through his role as the guide of souls to the underworld. In many myths, Mercury used his wit and diplomacy to guide souls safely to the realm of Pluto, navigating the complexities of the afterlife.

Celebrations and Honors

Mercury was honored throughout the Roman world. Those involved in commerce and trade were particularly prone to worship Mercury, as he was also considered the god of merchants. His ability to move swiftly and negotiate made him a patron deity for traders and businessmen.

The Romans celebrated the festival of *Mercuralia* on May 15th to honor Mercury. On this day, merchants would sprinkle their goods and their heads with water from a sacred well dedicated to Mercury, seeking his blessings for success in their ventures and protection in their travels.

Mercury's Legacy

Today, Mercury is remembered not only as a mythological figure but also as a symbol of communication. His legacy lives on in the term "mercurial," often used to describe someone who is witty, clever, and quick in thought and action. His influence is also evident in the medical symbol of the *caduceus*. The *caduceus* reflects Mercury's role as a healer and mediator.

All in all, Mercury's tales inspire us to be both quick in our actions and thoughtful in our decisions. Like Mercury, we should use our abilities to help and inform others.

Pluto: The Mysterious God of the Underworld

Now, let's head to the Underworld, where you can imagine a kingdom hidden beneath the earth filled from glittering minerals to the souls of the departed. All are kept safe under the watchful eye of Pluto. Pluto is a god often pictured with a stern face who holds the keys to the underworld. He is normally accompanied by Cerberus, the three-headed dog who guards the gates of his kingdom.

Like Jupiter, Pluto was the son of Saturn, the god of time, and Ops, the goddess of wealth. As such, he was also the brother of Jupiter and Neptune. While his brothers ruled the sky and the sea, Pluto's domain was the Underworld. There he reigned supreme, ensuring that the natural order of life and death was maintained.

Pluto's Kingdom

The Underworld was not just a place of darkness and gloom as many imagine. As the king of the underworld, Pluto was responsible for ensuring that the spirits of the dead found their rightful place, whether that was the peaceful fields of Elysium or the depths of Tartarus, depending on their deeds during life. This meant that the Romans believed that all spirits of the dead traveled to the Underworld after death.

In addition to being the god of the dead, Pluto was also associated with wealth, specifically the mineral riches of the earth like gold and silver. This connection likely came from the fact that these precious metals were mined underground. These minerals were considered gifts from Pluto himself. He also played a role in agriculture, which was tied to the belief that the seeds planted in the earth die to bring about new life. This belief mirrors the cycle of death and rebirth overseen by Pluto in the Underworld.

Pluto in Roman Myths

Pluto is featured in several Roman myths, most notably in the story of Proserpina (Persephone in Greek mythology). According to the myth, Pluto fell in love with Proserpina, the beautiful daughter of Ceres (goddess of agriculture). He abducted Proserpina to make her his queen in the Underworld. This act brought about the changing of the seasons. The myth attributes these changes to Ceres who, in her grief, caused all crops to wither until her daughter was allowed to return to the surface for part of the year.

Pluto's Legacy

Today, Pluto's name lives on in the dwarf planet Pluto, which was discovered in 1930. This small planet is a symbol of the fact there are mysterious and distant places in our solar system. Pluto's story also helps us understand the ancient Romans' views on life, death, and the natural world.

As you learn about Pluto, think of him not just as a dark, foreboding figure, but as a necessary part of the natural cycle of life. He reminds us that endings are just as important as beginnings, and that wealth and abundance can come from even the darkest of places.

Bellona: The Fierce Goddess of War

We end our journey through the action-packed world of Roman mythology, filled with gods and goddesses that oversaw various aspects of life and nature, with Bellona. This figure stood out as the formidable goddess of war. Known for her bravery and battle prowess, Bellona was a figure of strength and determination, inspiring soldiers and commanders as they headed into combat.

Bellona was closely associated with Mars, the god of war. As such, she was sometimes even considered to be his wife or sister. Together, they represented the full terror and valor of military conflict. While Mars was more broadly recognized as the deity of war strategy and masculinity, Bellona specifically symbolized actual warfare and its combative spirit. Before Roman soldiers went off to fight, they would often invoke her name in hopes she would grant them courage and victory. Bellona's temples served as places not only for worship, but also for planning military tactics and meetings among commanders.

Celebrating Bellona

Bellona was honored with several festivals and rituals, particularly by those about to embark on military campaigns. One of her most important celebrations was the Bellona Festival, held in June, which included parades and military displays. During this festival, soldiers and commanders gathered to pray for strength and victory in their upcoming battles.

Bellona's symbols, such as the helmet and weapons, underscored her "martial" nature. She also carried a torch or whip, which represented the harsh realities of war—destruction and discipline, respectively. These symbols made her a relatable and revered figure among those who faced the uncertainties of battle.

Bellona's Legacy

Today, Bellona's legacy can be seen in how we depict and remember female figures of war. Bellona embodies the idea that bravery and courage are not limited by gender, and that the spirit of battle resonates with the concept of the defense of one's home and values.

Chapter conclusion

Together, we've journeyed through the incredible legends and history of the Roman gods and goddesses. We have explored the powers and adventures of Jupiter, Juno, Neptune, and many others. Each story has shown us how these divine figures were thought to have influenced everything in Roman life, from the weather to the fate of the mighty Roman Empire. They weren't just characters in stories; they were symbols of strength, wisdom, and guidance, inspiring the people of ancient Rome.

CHAPTER 5: HEROES, LEGENDS & MYTHS THAT SHAPED ROME

In this last chapter, we'll dive into the captivating stories, myths and legends that helped shape ancient Rome. These myths served as more than just simple stories to the Romans. Rather, they were the backbone of Roman identity, offering lessons on morality, bravery, and the laws of the land. These stories have been passed down through generations, each one packed with drama, intrigue, and wisdom. Get ready to explore how these ancient myths influenced the great city of Rome and its people. Let's embark on this mythical journey together!

The Founding of Rome by Romulus and Remus

Long ago, in the misty realms of ancient history, legend has it that two twin brothers founded one of the greatest cities the world has ever known; Rome. This is the tale of Romulus and Remus, which mixes adventure, danger, and the fierce bonds of family. It is a myth that captures the imaginations of all who hear it.

The story begins with a princess named Rhea Silvia. She was the daughter of Numitor, the king of *Alba Longa*, a city near where Rome was eventually established. Numitor was overthrown by his cruel brother Amulius, who forced Rhea Silvia to become a Vestal Virgin (or, as mentioned previously, a priestess for the goddess of the home, Vesta). This new role meant she wasn't allowed to marry or have children. Mars, however, fell in love with her. So, she soon gave birth to twins, Romulus and Remus.

Fearing the boys would grow up to challenge him, Amulius ordered them to be thrown into the River Tiber. But destiny had other plans for these children, as the river god Tiberinus calmed the waters to save them. Because of Tiberinus, the basket carrying the twins came safely to rest in the soft mud of the riverbank.

Raised by a Wolf

Here, something wonderful happened. A she-wolf, hearing the cries of the infants, came to their rescue. She gently cared for them with her warm milk, a scene so touching that it would be remembered forever in the statues and paintings of Rome.

Later, a kind shepherd named Faustulus found the boys and brought them home. He and his wife, Acca Larentia, raised the boys as their own.

As the twins grew, they became natural leaders. Strong, brave, and fair, they attracted a band of loyal followers. As they learned of their royal heritage, however, the boys decided to overthrow Amulius and restore their grandfather, Numitor, to the throne of Alba Longa. After achieving this, Romulus and Remus set out to build a city of their own.

Founding a New City

The brothers chose a spot near the River Tiber, where they had been saved as infants, to establish their new city. But soon, a fierce argument broke out between them. Both wanted to rule the city and to decide its location and name. To resolve this problem, Romulus and Remus agreed to seek the gods' favor through a contest of *augury* (which was how Romans interpreted the will of the gods by looking at how birds flew).

As ancient Rome was said to have been built on seven hills, each brother chose one to stand on. Romulus stood on Palatine Hill and Remus on Aventine Hill. They chose these hills to practice *augury* and looked for flying birds. Where Remus only saw six birds, Romulus saw twelve. Thus, the supporters of Romulus claimed this as a sign that the gods favored him as the new ruler, and that the Palatine Hill should be the site of the new city.

The dispute over the omens led to more arguments. One day, in a fit of anger, Romulus killed Remus. Though he was heartbroken, Romulus went on to build the city. He named it Rome after himself, becoming its first king and establishing many of its laws and traditions.

Rome grew rapidly under Romulus. He invited people from all walks of life to become its citizens, creating a melting pot of cultures that made the city strong and vibrant. He also formed the Roman Senate, laying the foundations for what would become a great republic and then an even greater empire.

Conclusion

The tale of Romulus and Remus is more than just an origin story for Rome; it's a narrative about destiny, leadership, and the complexities of human nature. It teaches us that actions have consequences, being compassionate is important, and strong foundations have an enduring impact. The story of these twin brothers continues to fascinate and remind us that great beginnings often come from humble origins.

The Horatii and Curiatii: A Tale of Honor and Sacrifice

After the establishment of Rome, the city thrived alongside its neighbor, Alba Longa. As often happens between neighbors, tensions rose, and soon they were on the brink of war. But instead of leading their people into a bloody battle, the leaders decided that the conflict should be settled by a duel between two sets of triplets; the Horatii brothers from Rome and the Curiatii brothers from Alba Longa.

The Horatii and the Curiatii were chosen as the strongest and bravest young men in their respective cities. Each was determined to bring victory to their respective city.. On the day of the duel, the six young men met on the battlefield. They would fight under the watchful eyes of their fellow citizens, who gathered to witness this unusual contest that would decide their fate.

The Battle Begins

The battle was fierce and evenly matched at first. As the brothers' swords clashed,tension among the spectators was noticeable. Before long, however, the tide of battle turned. Two of the Horatii were struck down, while all three Curiatii were wounded. It seemed that Alba Longa was destined to win, as only one Horatius brother remained standing against three injured Curiatii.

A Clever Strategy

But the last Horatius, knowing he couldn't defeat all three Curiatii in a direct flight, came up with a clever plan. He pretended to flee, hoping to separate his slower, wounded opponents. As expected, the Curiatii, hindered by their injuries, chased after him at different speeds. This caused them to spread out across the field. Turning swiftly, Horatius faced them one by one in single combat, using his full strength against their weakened states. This strategy was successful; he defeated each Curiatius brother separately, securing a dramatic and hard-won victory for Rome.

After the Battle

When Horatius returned to Rome, he was hailed as a hero. However, the story took a tragic turn when he discovered his sister weeping. She had been betrothed to one of the Curiatii, and her grief overwhelmed her. In a moment of anger and sorrow, Horatius killed his sister, declaring that no Roman should mourn an enemy of the state. This act shocked the city. As such, Horatius was put on trial for his sister's murder.

In the end, he was set free, largely due to his recent service to Rome. The Horatius brother, however, was required to pass under a yoke as a symbol of atonement for his crime. The yoke served to remind him of the heavy burden of his actions.

The Legacy of the Horatii and Curiatii

The duel between the Horatii and Curiatii became a legendary part of Roman heritage, teaching lessons about the gravity of war and the honor of warriors. It showed that sometimes, the greatest battles are not won by strength alone, but by cleverness, courage, and a deep sense of duty.

Aeneas's Big Journey: The Founding Hero of Rome

Aeneas was a Trojan prince that was known for his strength and bravery. As previously mentioned, he was also said to be the son of Venus. That meant he was half-human, half-god. During the Trojan War, Aeneas fought valiantly to defend his city. Troy, however, was destined to fall. As the city burned, Aeneas gathered his family and a group of followers and fled. To make sure everyone escaped, Aeneas carried his elderly father on his back and led his son by the hand.

After escaping Troy, Aeneas and his followers began a long and perilous journey across the sea in search of a new home. This mission was not just about survival; it was a divine quest assigned to Aeneas by the gods. They told him that he would establish a new city that would one day grow into a great empire. Unsurprisingly, this city was Rome.

Aeneas's voyage was filled with challenges and adventures. One of his first stops was at a city called Carthage, where a beautiful queen named Dido fell in love with him. They shared a brief, happy time together, but Aeneas knew he couldn't stay. After the gods reminded Aeneas of his destiny, he left Carthage with a heavy heart, also causing Dido to be heartbroken.

As Aeneas continued his journey, he and his crew faced many dangers, including a terrifying encounter with a cyclops and a journey to the Underworld. In the Underworld, however, Aeneas met the spirit of his father. His father showed Aeneas the long line of descendants who would follow him and the great city they would build.

The Arrival in Italy

Finally, after many years of traveling, Aeneas and his followers reached the shores of Italy. But, their trials were not over yet. They had to fight several fierce battles against local tribes who did not welcome the newcomers. Still, with his leadership and the help of the gods, Aeneas was able to secure a piece of land where they could settle.

Aeneas's journey did not just lead to the founding of a new city; it set the stage for the creation of the Roman Empire. Aeneas was seen by the Romans as a model of piety and duty, always putting his obligations above his personal desires. His story was immortalized by the poet Virgil in the epic poem "The Aeneid," which became a national epic of Rome.

Aeneas's big journey teaches us about the importance of perseverance and following one's destiny. It shows that even when the path is filled with obstacles, determination and faith can lead to great things. Finally, Aeneas's adventures remind us that even from small beginnings, great empires can grow.

Cincinnatus: The Farmer Who Saved Rome

Though many heroes shaped the city of Rome's destiny with their courage and wisdom, Lucius Quinctius Cincinnatus stands out as a true model of selflessness and duty. His story is not just a tale of heroism in battle, but also a lesson in humility and the virtues of simplicity. Let's explore how this humble farmer came to save Rome and became one of its greatest legends.

Cincinnatus was a simple Roman farmer who lived in the early days of the Roman Republic, around the 5th century BC. He owned a small plot of land, which he tended with his own hands. He lived a simple life, but those who knew him for his integrity and wisdom respected him greatly.

A City in Crisis

The story of Cincinnatus begins with a crisis in Rome, as the city was under threat from neighboring tribes.At that moment, the Roman army was trapped and the enemy was closing in. It was apparent that Rome needed a leader who could guide them through this perilous time. The Roman

Senate knew exactly whom to call upon – Cincinnatus, known for his previous service as a consul and his unquestionable moral character.

According to legend, messengers sent by the Senate found Cincinnatus at his farm, plowing the fields. They approached him with great reverence and told him that Rome needed him to become dictator. This was a powerful role given only in times of emergency and allowed the leader to have complete control over the city to handle the crisis. Cincinnatus accepted the responsibility without hesitation, leaving his plow in the fields and heading to the city to take command.

Once in power, Cincinnatus acted swiftly. He organized the troops, devised a brilliant plan, and led the army to battle himself. With cunning strategy and fearless leadership, he defeated the enemy. Then, Cincinnatus rescued the trapped Roman soldiers and returned triumphantly to Rome—all within a mere 15 days.

A True Hero's Choice

What Cincinnatus did next is what truly made him a legend. Instead of using his power to enrich himself or extend his rule, he did something almost unheard of—he resigned and returned to his farm. Cincinnatus had been granted absolute power to save Rome, but once he had done so, he willingly gave that power up. This act of selflessness and devotion to the Republic made him a symbol of civic virtue and duty.

Cincinnatus's Legacy

Cincinnatus became a hero not only for his military deeds but also for his character. His story has been told throughout the centuries as an example of leadership at its best—power used wisely and relinquished willingly for the common good. Cincinnatus teaches us that true leadership involves putting the needs of one's community or country before their own desires.

The Legend of the Capitoline Geese

Throughout Roman history, many humans have been recognized as heroes. Atop the Capitoline Hill, however, appears a different tale—or, that of few feathered heroes whose vigilance saved the city from disaster.

This is the story of the Capitoline geese. These birds were not a flock not of mighty eagles or a pride of fierce lions, but rather a group of simple, watchful geese who became unsung heroes of Rome. Their legend is a delightful blend of how small creatures can make a big difference and that even the most unlikely heroes can save the day.

A City Under Siege

The story takes us back to a time when Rome was under siege by the fierce Gauls in 390 BC. The Gauls were led by their chieftain Brennus. The Romans were struggling to defend their city against these powerful invaders who had already captured much of the city. The only place left unconquered was Capitoline Hill, a fortified area and the last refuge for the city's defenders.

The Gauls knew that taking the Capitoline Hill would mean victory. So, they tried every trick to capture it. At first, the Gauls fought hard during the day but could not break through the Roman defenses. So, they devised a cunning plan to climb the hill's cliffs under the cover of night and catch the Romans off-guard while they slept.

The Night of the Climbing Gauls

So, one dark night, the Gauls began their silent climb up the steep cliffs of Capitoline Hill. The Roman guards, weary after days of siege, didn't notice the silent shadows inching closer to the city's last stronghold. It seemed that nothing could stop the Gauls from overrunning the hill and sealing Rome's fate.

The Geese Spring into Action

One important detail of Capitoline Hill was forgotten, however, which were : the sacred geese of Juno. This flock was housed in her temple on the hill. As these were not ordinary geese (they were devoted to Juno, the goddess who watched over the city), they perhaps had a touch of her divine awareness.

As the Gauls neared the top, the geese sensed something amiss. They began honking furiously, flapping their wings and creating a racket that no human guard had managed. Startled by the noise, Marcus Manlius, a former consul and a vigilant defender of Rome, woke up. He quickly gathered other soldiers to rush towards the noise.

The Battle on the Hill

The Romans arrived just in time to see the shadowy figures of the Gauls reaching the top of the cliffs. Thanks to the geese's warnings, the Romans were prepared and fought fiercely. They managed to push the surprised Gauls back down the hill, thwarting their night attack. The geese had saved Capitoline Hill—and Rome itself—with their watchful eyes and loud warning.

The next day, as the story of the night's events spread throughout the remaining Roman forces. The geese were hailed as heroes as they had succeeded in detecting the silent approach of the Gauls even when the guards had failed to do so. The grateful Romans saw this as a sign that Juno herself was protecting the city through her sacred birds.

Legacy of the Legend

The Legend of the Capitoline Geese became a cherished tale among the Romans. As such, Juno's geese were celebrated in sculptures and stories, and they became a symbol of watchfulness and protection in Roman culture.

This is a tale that encourages us to be vigilant and courageous. Most importantly, however, it teaches us to appreciate the everyday heroes in our lives, whether they have feathers, fur, or two hands.

The Tale of Mucius Scaevola: The Brave, Left-Handed Hero

Though Juno's geese were essential to Rome's survival of the Gauls, let's get back to human heroes. Long ago, a young man named Mucius, who would come to be known as Mucius Scaevola (which means "Mucius the Left-Handed"), made his mark on ancient Rome. This legend not only thrilled the people of Rome, but also taught them the value of courage and conviction.

A City Under Siege

Mucius's story begins when the city of Rome was under siege by a fierce king named Lars Porsena and his people, the Etruscans. Due to the king's mighty army, Rome seemed on the brink of defeat. This worried the Romans, who feared their beloved city might fall into the hands of the enemy. But amid these dark times, young Mucius, a mere citizen with no great title or rank, decided he would do something to save his city.

Mucius came up with a bold plan: he would sneak into the enemy camp and assassinate King Lars Porsena himself. He believed that without their leader, the enemy army would be thrown into chaos and retreat. With his heart set on saving Rome, Mucius bid farewell to his family and friends and slipped into the enemy camp, disguised as an Etruscan soldier.

The Mistake and the Test

Mucius tried to find the king in the bustling camp. In a fateful mix-up, however, he mistook the king's scribe for the king himself. Mucius killed the scribe instead, meaning he was immediately captured by the soldiers and brought before King Porsena. The king was furious and demanded to know why Mucius had attempted such a bold act.

Standing before the king, Mucius showed no fear. He declared proudly that he was a Roman and that many other brave Romans were ready to risk their lives to protect their city just as he had. To prove his courage and that fear had no hold on him, Mucius thrust his right hand into a nearby fire. He burned it without showing any signs of pain, shocking everyone including King Porsena.

The King's Response

Moved by Mucius's courage and realizing the determination of the Roman people, King Porsena decided to negotiate peace rather than continue the war. He was impressed by the young Roman's bravery and saw that the spirit of Rome was stronger and more resilient than he had thought. Mucius was freed without harm, and he returned to Rome a hero.

Upon his return, Mucius was given the nickname "Scaevola," meaning "left-handed," because his right hand had been disabled by the fire. He was honored by all of Rome, and his deed became a symbol of the bravery that every Roman was expected to embody. Mucius's story was told and retold, inspiring countless others to be courageous in the face of danger.

The tale of Mucius Scaevola is more than just a story of a young man who dared to defend his city; it's a lesson in the power of courage and the strength of conviction. It teaches us that sometimes, one brave act can change the course of history. Mucius reminds us that true heroism comes from standing firm for what we believe in, no matter the odds.

The Story of Cloelia: The Brave Roman Girl

Though many heroes woven into the rich tapestry of Roman legends were men, let's talk about a brave young girl named Cloelia. Unlike tales of warriors and kings, Cloelia's story is a remarkable testament to the bravery and resourcefulness of youth. Her adventure not only inspired the hearts of ancient Romans but continues to teach us about courage and cleverness today.

A City in Peril

This tale begins during the same troubling time for Rome as when Mucius had lived. The city was at war with a neighboring state, Clusium, ruled by the fierce King Lars Porsena. In an attempt to secure peace, the Romans agreed to send hostages to King Porsena. Among these hostages was a young girl named Cloelia.

Cloelia, along with other Roman youths, was taken to the enemy camp across the Tiber River. While life in the camp was safe and the hostages were treated well, the idea of being prisoners weighed heavily on them. They longed for their freedom and their beloved city, but escape seemed impossible. The hostages were closely guarded and surrounded by the wide, rushing river.

Cloelia's Bold Plan

Cloelia was not one to sit by idly. She devised a daring plan to escape and lead her fellow hostages back to Rome. With a spirit as fierce as any warrior's, Cloelia rallied the other young Romans and led them to the river's edge. Under the cover of darkness, they made their bold move.

Cloelia was aware that the river served as a formidable barrier, but she also knew it was the hostages' only path to freedom. With courage in their hearts, Cloelia and the hostages plunged into the Tiber and began to swim across its swift currents. It was a perilous journey and not all were strong swimmers. Still, Cloelia urged them on with unyielding determination.

Against all odds, Cloelia and her companions reached the far bank of the river. Wet and weary, but excited by their success, the hostages made their way back to Rome. Their return was met with joy and astonishment. Cloelia was hailed as a heroine and all of Rome celebrated her bravery.

King Porsena was furious when he learned of the hostages' escape. He demanded that Cloelia be sent back to him, as per the terms of the peace treaty. The Romans, bound by honor, agreed. So, Cloelia returned to the Clusian camp, bravely facing the consequences of her actions.

Impressed by her courage and integrity, King Porsena did something unexpected—he forgave Cloelia and praised her bravery. As a token of his admiration, he allowed Cloelia to choose half of the remaining hostages to take back with her to Rome. So, Cloelia chose the youngest, and once again, she returned to her city. This time, however, she was not an escapee, but rather a negotiator of freedom.

The story of Cloelia teaches us that bravery comes in many forms, and even the youngest among us can change the course of history with acts of great courage. Her tale reminds us to stand up for what we believe in. Cloelia reminds us that the greatest heroes are those who act not only for themselves but for the good of others.

Wisdom from the Waters

After the fierce and mighty Romulus established Rome, there came a king who was his opposite in nearly every way. This king was Numa Pompilius, a wise and thoughtful ruler who sought to enrich Rome with laws and rituals instead of expanding the city through battle. One of the most enchanting tales from his reign is that of his secret advisor, Egeria. This story is a beautiful example of how ancient

Romans revered both wisdom and nature, and the tale speaks to the power of knowledge and peace.

As the story goes, Numa would often wander the forests near Rome, seeking solitude and space to think about the laws he was creating for his people. During one of these walks, he encountered the nymph Egeria. Egeria was a wise and beautiful nymph who lived in a sacred grove with springs and streams that were said to have healing properties.

Egeria, impressed by Numa's dedication to his city and his kind heart, decided to help him. She became his advisor, meeting him in the grove where she lived. To hide her existence, she counseled Numa under the cover of night. During their talks, Egeria shared her divine knowledge of rituals, laws, and governance with Numa. With Egeria's counsel, Numa established many of the religious customs and institutions that would shape Roman society for centuries to come.

Thanks to Egeria's wisdom and Numa's leadership, Rome enjoyed a long period of peace and prosperity. Numa set up colleges for priests, including the Vestal Virgins, and created the Pontifex Maximus. The Pontifex Maximus was the high priest who oversaw all religious ceremonies to ensure that the gods continued to support Rome.

Numa's laws were just and aimed at maintaining peace and fairness in Roman society. He believed this structure pleased the gods and brought stability. The king's focus on law and rituals deeply ingrained the importance of religion in Roman public life, and taught the Romans that peace was just as honorable as war.

The Legacy of Numa and Egeria

The tale of Numa Pompilius and the nymph Egeria teaches us that it is important to seek knowledge from those who can share it. It shows that true leadership involves listening, learning, and respecting both the people and the world around us. Their story is a beautiful reminder of how peace can lead to a society's prosperity and how nature can inspire the best in us all.

Chapter Conclusion

Now, we have ventured through the captivating myths that not only entertained the citizens of ancient Rome and grounded them in values and principles that defined their civilization. These stories, rich with heroes and moral lessons, have painted a vivid picture of the societal ideals and spiritual beliefs that influenced everything from daily life to grand policy in ancient Rome.

As we close this chapter, we carry with us the timeless wisdom and enduring spirit of these ancient legends. The tales of courage, sacrifice, and innovation continue to inspire us and remind us of how myth has the power to shape societies and moral landscapes.

CONCLUSION

As we reach the end of our journey through "Roman Legends for Kids," we remember the grandeur, the triumphs, and the eventual fall of one of the most iconic civilizations in history—the Roman Empire. Its decline, marked by the relentless Barbarian invasions, severe economic troubles, and the division into East and West, teaches us about the vulnerability of even the mightiest powers when faced with internal and external pressures.

Throughout the book, we have traveled back in time to explore bustling marketplaces, stood in the shadows of colossal aqueducts, and heard the roaring crowds of the Colosseum. We met formidable emperors who strategized Rome's expansions, brave gladiators who fought for glory and freedom, and inventive gods and goddesses who shaped the fates of people and cities alike.

Each legend and historical figure has taught us about courage, wisdom, and the complexities of human nature. From the strategic prowess of Julius Caesar to the architectural innovations that still influence modern engineering, the legacy of Rome is a testament to the empire's lasting impact on law, language, and governance that still resonates in our world today.

But, you should consider this book as only the beginning of your adventure into the past. History is filled with mysteries waiting to be solved and stories yearning to be heard. By exploring archaeology, engaging with storytelling, and studying the histories of ancient civilizations like Rome, you can discover how the past shapes our present and influences our future.

So, keep the spirit of curiosity alive! Visit museums, read more books, and discuss what you've learned with friends and family. Perhaps one day, you will add your own stories to the rich tapestry of history.

Remember that every chapter of history offers insights that can inspire and guide us. Let these tales of Rome remind you that you, too, can build something enduring that might one day inspire future generations. So, turn the page and start creating your own chapter to add to the book of history! Whether you're just getting started or you're ready to challenge yourself further, remember to keep discovering new things and bringing history to life!

Congratulations on completing your grand tour through the legends of ancient Rome! Head over to the quiz section and see how much you've learned. Can you answer all the questions and prove yourself to be a young historian of Rome?

TEST YOUR KNOWLEDGE

Hey young explorers! Now that you've journeyed through the grand stories of ancient Rome, met mighty emperors and courageous gladiators, learned about powerful gods and legendary heroes, how much can you remember? It's time to put your knowledge to the test with this fun quiz. Ready to prove that you're a true historian of ancient Rome?

Let's get started!

Chapter 1: Mighty Emperors of Rome

Who was known as the founder of the Roman Empire?

- A) Caligula
- B) Nero
- C) Augustus
- D) Tiberius

Which emperor is famous for his philosophical writings and being a "Philosopher-Emperor?"

- A) Nero
- B) Julius Caesar
- C) Marcus Aurelius
- D) Vespasian

Name the emperor who famously made his horse a senator.

- A) Nero
- B) Caligula
- C) Claudius
- D) Diocletian

Who was the emperor during the Great Fire of Rome in AD 64?

- A) Vespasian
- B) Titus
- C) Nero
- D) Domitian

Which emperor divided the Roman Empire into the Eastern and Western Roman Empires?

- A) Constantine the Great
- B) Julian
- C) Diocletian
- D) Theodosius I

Chapter 2: Powerful Women of Rome

Who was Livia Drusilla?

- A) The mother of Nero
- B) The confidante and advisor to her husband, Emperor Augustus
- C) A famous Roman poet
- D) The last queen of Rome

Name the queen who allied with both Julius Caesar and Mark Antony.

- A) Agrippina the Younger
- B) Julia Domna
- C) Cleopatra VII
- D) Livia Drusilla

Which warrior queen led a revolt against Roman invasion in her territory?

- A) Julia Domna
- B) Boudica
- C) Fulvia
- D) Cleopatra VII

Who was the mother of Emperor Nero and a prominent figure in Roman politics?

- A) Agrippina the Younger
- B) Cleopatra VII
- C) Livia Drusilla
- D) Julia Domna

Name the Roman empress known for her philosophical interests and support of her son's reign.

- A) Agrippina the Younger
- B) Julia Domna
- C) Cleopatra VII
- D) Boudica

Chapter 3: Brave Gladiators of the Colosseum

Who was the gladiator that led a major slave uprising against Rome?

- A) Tetraites
- B) Commodus
- C) Spartacus
- D) Crixus

What type of gladiator was known for using a net and trident?

- A) Murmillo
- B) Retiarius
- C) Secutor
- D) Thraex

Which two gladiators were known for their battle that ended in a draw, earning them both their freedom?

- A) Flamma and Crixus
- B) Spartacus and Commodus
- C) Priscus and Verus
- D) Tetraites and Secutor

What was the name of the gladiator who refused to win his freedom, choosing to remain in the arena instead?

- A) Commodus
- B) Flamma
- C) Crixus
- D) Spartacus

Chapter 4: Mighty Gods & Goddesses of Rome

Who was the king of the Roman gods?

- A) Mars
- B) Saturn
- C) Jupiter
- D) Neptune

Name the god of the sea in Roman mythology.

- A) Mars
- B) Mercury
- C) Neptune
- D) Pluto

Which goddess is associated with love and beauty?

- A) Juno
- B) Vesta
- C) Bellona
- D) Venus

Who was the Roman god of war, also associated with agriculture?

- A) Mars
- B) Vulcan
- C) Mercury
- D) Saturn

Chapter 5: Heroes, Legends & Myths that Shaped Rome

Which is the legendary story of the founding of Rome?

- A) The journey of Aeneas
- B) The tale of Mucius Scaevola
- C) The founding by Romulus and Remus
- D) The legend of Cincinnatus

Who was the hero believed to have journeyed from Troy to establish the city ofRome?

- A) Julius Caesar
- B) Romulus
- C) Aeneas
- D) Remus

Name the Roman hero who is known for sticking his hand in a fire to prove his bravery.

- A) Cincinnatus
- B) Mucius Scaevola
- C) Numa Pompilius
- D) Gaius Mucius Cordus

Which Roman figure is celebrated for returning to his farm after saving Rome from invasion?

- A) Cincinnatus
- B) Aeneas
- C) Gaius Mucius Cordus
- D) Romulus

Who were the twin brothers who fought against each other to settle a war between Alba Longa and Rome?

- A) Aeneas and Ascanius
- B) Romulus and Remus
- C) The Horatii and Curiatii
- D) Priscus and Verus

ANSWERS

Chapter 1: Mighty Emperors of Rome

Who was known as the founder of the Roman Empire?

Answer: C) Augustus

Which emperor is famous for his philosophical writings and being a "Philosopher_Emperor?"

Answer: C) Marcus Aurelius

Name the emperor who famously made his horse a senator.

Answer: B) Caligula

Who was the emperor during the Great Fire of Rome in AD 64?

Answer: C) Nero

Which emperor divided the Roman Empire into the Eastern and Western Roman Empires?

Answer: C) Diocletian

Chapter 2: Powerful Women of Rome

Who was Livia Drusilla?

Answer: B) The confidante and advisor to her husband, Emperor Augustus

Name the queen who allied with both Julius Caesar and Mark Antony.

Answer: C) Cleopatra VII

Which warrior queen led a revolt against Roman invasion in her territory?

Answer: B) Boudica

Who was the mother of Emperor Nero and a prominent figure in Roman politics?

Answer: A) Agrippina the Younger

Name the Roman empress known for her philosophical interests and support of her son's reign.

Answer: B) Julia Domna

Chapter 3: Brave Gladiators of the Colosseum

Who was the gladiator that led a major slave uprising against Rome?

Answer: C) Spartacus

What type of gladiator was known for using a net and trident?

Answer: B) Retiarius

Which two gladiators were known for their battle that ended in a draw, earning them both their freedom?

Answer: C) Priscus and Verus

What was the name of the gladiator who refused to win his freedom, choosing to remain in the arena instead?

Answer: B) Flamma

Chapter 4: Mighty Gods & Goddesses of Rome

Who was the king of the Roman gods?

Answer: C) Jupiter

Name the god of the sea in Roman mythology.

Answer: C) Neptune

Which goddess is associated with love and beauty?

Answer: D) Venus

Who was the Roman god of war, also associated with agriculture?

Answer: A) Mars

Chapter 5: Heroes, Legends & Myths that Shaped Rome

Which is the legendary story of the founding of Rome?

Answer: C) The founding by Romulus and Remus

Who was the hero believed to have journeyed from Troy to establish the city of Rome?

Answer: C) Aeneas

Name the Roman hero who is known for sticking his hand in fire to prove his bravery.

Answer: B) Mucius Scaevola

Which Roman figure is celebrated for returning to his farm after saving Rome from invasion?

Answer: A) Cincinnatus

Who were the twin brothers who fought against each other to settle a war between Alba Longa and Rome?

Answer: C) The Horatii and Curiatii

REFERENCES

This book was created using sources including books, academic journals, educational websites, encyclopedias, documentaries, and museum collections to provide a thorough and engaging exploration of ancient Roman history, culture, and mythology.

Books:

- "The History of Rome" by Titus Livius (Livy)
- "SPQR: A History of Ancient Rome" by Mary Beard
- "The Oxford Classical Dictionary"
- "Encyclopedia Britannica"

Academic Journals and Articles:

- Journal of Roman Studies
- Classical Antiquity
- JSTOR
- Google Scholar

Educational:

- BBC History
- National Geographic Kids
- TED-Ed videos on Roman history, which are often created and vetted by educators and can provide both inspiration and factual content.
- The British Museum
- The Metropolitan Museum of Art